To Georgia,

Love, joy and peace

Gudrun Spell 1998

A Time to Laugh
A Time to Weep

History Experienced: My Childhood
Memories of Growing Up During
the Third Reich, World War II, and
Foreign Military Occupations

Gudrun M. Gsell

Baltimore, Maryland

A Time to Laugh, A Time to Weep

Library of Congress
Cataloging in Publication Data
ISBN 1-56167-397-8

Library of Congress Card Catalog Number:
97-075534

Published by

Noble House

8019 Belair Road, Suite 10
Baltimore, Maryland 21236

Manufactured in the United States of America

I dedicate this book to my beloved family:
My husband, William
My children, Christin, Eric, and Constance
My grandchildren, Teresa and Bryan

And to all the millions who have suffered
through and remember the horrors of war.

"For everything there is a season
And a time for everything under heaven:

A time to be born and a time to die;
A time to plant and a time to reap;
A time to kill and a time to heal; . . .
A time to weep and a time to laugh; . . .
A time to love and a time to hate;
A time for war and a time for peace."

Ecclesiastes 3

Gudrun, ready to leave for college in the U.S.A.

Leaving My Homeland, Germany

It was midnight when we arrived in Le Havre, France. The boat train had left Stuttgart, my hometown, twenty-three hours before. We had a seven hour layover in Paris, enough time to do some sightseeing.

In spite of the cool weather and drizzling rain, I thoroughly enjoyed visiting the Arche de Triumphe, the Eiffel Tower, St. Madeleine's Church, Napoleon's Tomb and other tourist attractions.

My parents took me to the train station in Stuttgart where we had to wait and wait for the special train that would transport us to Le Havre. The crowd was a mixture of American citizens returning home, emigrants, and displaced persons from Eastern Europe, young German brides of American servicemen, and students who were allowed to study in the USA for one year.

I had already finished the first part of my college work in

Germany. I was now classified as an Early Childhood Educator. I had finished two years of college and three years of practical work with children of different ages. This included teaching, nursing, working in a maternity ward and children's hospital, as well as day care and being a governess with a Swiss family.

I needed an additional two years of practical work before I could return to college for two more years of study. After that I would receive my Master's Degree in Developmental Psychology.

That was my plan; however, my dream for years had been to visit America or to study there. I applied, and to my great joy I received a scholarship to the University of Indianapolis.

And here I was traveling all by myself to this big, promising land. Passport, visa for one year, and scholarship papers in hand, I also possessed a ticket for passage on the most luxurious floating palace, the S. S. United States. The day was August 24, 1954.

The train stopped in Le Havre. It was midnight, dark and dreary. All passengers disembarked and headed for the pier. What a sight, what a most dazzling sight. There she was, expecting her passengers. Outlined by hundreds of brilliant lights, this glorious ship welcomed us.

I put down my hand luggage and gazed at this marvel. In my excitement I let out a shout of pure joy and wonderment. I knew that this sight was an omen of the life awaiting me in the United States. Good-bye, ruined cities! Good-bye memories of war, death, hunger and misery! I was leaving for the PROMISED LAND!

I had studied British English in high school, beginning at age ten. It was my favorite subject. After the war I was able to translate the correspondence Father had with Americans. Now I could use this knowledge on the ship. It was good practice. Most of the ship's crew spoke French and German as well as English.

Was this reality or just a wonderful dream from which I did not want to wake, ever?

I finally found my cabin. Two older ladies besides me

occupied our sleeping quarters. Being the youngest I, of course, was asked to take the upper bunk. I did not mind.

After enjoying a brief meal, everyone settled down for the night. I was too excited to sleep, so I went to the top deck and stood there, looking out over the harbor. I listened to the gentle splashing of the waves against the sparkling white hull until I heard the ship's engines starting to rumble. It was three o'clock in the morning. The golden moon peeked out from behind silver-edged, puffy clouds as if wishing us a safe voyage.

I suddenly realized that I had passed the "point of no return." Europe would soon be behind me, the Atlantic Ocean was before me, and at the end of the voyage lay New York. As we steamed through the rough waters of the English Channel, we passed the black ruins of former bunkers, rusty burnt-out tanks and twisted piles of barbed wire along the sandy beaches of the Normandy.

They were ghostly reminders of the Allied Forces' invasion on June 6, 1944—D Day. Countless brave soldiers on both sides, friend and foe, sacrificed their young lives at Normandy, far away from home. "Lord, have mercy on their souls," I prayed.

I grew up during the Third Reich, suffered through, and survived World War II as well as foreign military occupation of my homeland. As I was standing on the ship's deck in the darkness of night, my mind wandered back to my childhood years, and many half forgotten memories suddenly became crystal clear as the ship slowly slipped away from the French coast. I decided then to write, in addition to my war diary, about the many experiences which will always be part of my life.

The world I grew up in is no more, changed forever, but not forgotten.

History, Customs, and Childhood Stories

My parents' wedding day, April 29, 1926. Lydia Wintterle and Karl Leonhard.

My Hometown, Stuttgart

For thousands of years the valley of the Neckar and Rems rivers was home to ancient tribes. Its fertile soil, surrounding forested hills, and grassy slopes were ideal for homesteading. Agriculture developed even before the Romans established farms in this pleasant valley over two thousand years ago. Vineyards planted by these early settlers are still being tended on the terraced hillsides.

Mosaic floors and Roman baths have recently been excavated and ancient coins discovered. Stuttgart's "Roemerstrasse" (Roman Street) was the first cobblestone road found in the area, and it is still in use. The name Stuttgart means "Mares' Garden" and is witness to the valley being home to domesticated horse breeding farms. The city's crest is still a black rearing mare on a yellow background.

The hilltop keeps a special treasure. Among the ancient beech and oak trees, one can find a linden tree which is said to be well over one thousand years old. This tree is circled by simple stone seats worn by weather, and many a weary wanderer has rested there. The linden tree and its surroundings is where, centuries ago, rulers held the "Ting," the court of elders belonging to ancient Germanic tribes. Here laws were made and criminals judged.

Carved wooden beech sticks were used to decide the guilt or innocence of the accused. The judge gathered the sticks in his right fist, dropped them to the ground, and the group of respected elders observed the design the sticks made on the ground. If they fell all in one heap, the accused was found guilty. If they scattered neatly in a circle the accused was freed.

Stuttgart Gothic Cathedral (Stiftskirche)

This was the custom before written language was developed. Later these sticks were put in certain order to form letters like the A, E, K, and M shapes we still use today. The German word for "letter of the alphabet" is *buchstabe*. In English its meaning is "beech staff."

In the ninth century a monastery and a Romanesque church were built in the valley. These buildings were the beginning of Stuttgart's growth into a city. Surrounding the monastery, craftsmen settled to tend to the needs of the monks. Shoemakers, bakers, butchers, tailors and many others were needed. One tower of the early church is still standing and bears the year of its completion—Anno Domini 908. The monastery was in use until the Reformation in the sixteenth century, when by Royal Decree the state of Wuerttemberg, with Stuttgart as its capital, became Protestant. Wuerttemberg, even today, is mostly Lutheran, while Bavaria to the East is mainly Catholic.

In its beginning Stuttgart was a walled city. Inside the citizens were protected from enemy attacks. Everyone had to be home before nightfall when the heavy city gates were locked with huge keys. On each corner of the city wall, a watch tower was erected and guarded day and night.

The leper colony was located outside the city. This terribly feared and disfiguring illness was rampant during the Thirty Years War, 1616-1646. When those unfortunate individuals who were stricken by leprosy wanted to enter the city, they had to be covered from head to toe with robes. This included their faces. Only slits around their eyes were permitted. The lepers had to carry small bells, which they rang as a warning to healthy citizens.

Sundials first measured daytime. Some of the very old church towers still show sundials bearing Roman Numerals. During the last few centuries, large clocks were installed along with the sundials. The night watchman had to call out the hours between 10:00 p.m. and 6:00 a.m., and I remember a few of the verses he sang long ago:

> *Listen, Masters, let me tell you*
> *Our clock has just struck ten.*
> *Ten commandments God has given.*
> *Be obedient to all of them.*

> *Listen, Masters, let me tell you*
> *Our clock eleven has struck.*
> *Eleven disciples faithful remained.*
> *One became a traitor vile.*

> *Listen, Masters, let me tell you*
> *Our clock has just struck twelve.*
> *Twelve is the fulfillment of time.*
> *Mankind, consider eternal life.*

> *Listen, Masters, let me tell you*
> *Our clock has just struck one.*
> *One God only rules the world.*
> *He will protect us from evil and harm.*

So it went all night until sunrise. I remember as a child

standing before the Monument to the Night Watchman. It still stands in front of the St. Leonhard's Church. He carries a lantern in one hand and a lance in the other. His shoulders are covered by a long cape. His mouth is open as if he were singing his message to a sleeping city. I have often wondered what life might have been long ago when Stuttgart was still a small town.

The only person during my childhood who reminded me of the night watchman was the man who lit our gas lights every night as he walked up and down the streets in our neighborhood. Soon the gaslights were replaced by electric bulbs. They turned off and on automatically.

Before World War II broke out, I well remember the excitement one day when the big airship, the Hindenburg, floated across Stuttgart. Many curious neighbors gathered in the small scenic lookout, which was a landscaped little park shaded by locust trees. We children often played there during outings with our nursemaid, Ellie. Other nannies visited this park as well with their charges. The children played in the sand or rode their tricycles while the nannies sat on the benches and chatted with one another. I loved playing with these babies and toddlers. I have always enjoyed young children.

But the afternoon when the airship—also called a zeppelin— arrived, the nannies were nowhere in sight. In their stead adults and older children flocked to the lookout to see this wonder of early air travel honoring our city with a visit. The gray, helium-filled, "balloon-like" upper part looked to me like a giant whale. The tiny gondola for passengers seemed like a fin. Yes, this vehicle really looked like a flying whale. It quietly floated across the city and then it was gone.

During World War II the city was almost totally bombed-out. From the same little park where we observed the zeppelin, we saw nothing but stone ruins. After the war, the city fathers tried to recycle the ruins by grinding all stone, mortar, sand and other materials and shaping them into new building blocks, but to their disappointment, it could not be done. So, for years truck companies were obliged to spend one day a week helping with the clearing of roads and properties. Outside the city a Hill of

Ruins was constructed. When all the cleaning-up was finished, a road was built up the hill, trees were planted, and now the Hill of Ruins blends into the rest of the forested hillsides of Stuttgart. Three crosses were erected on a plateau topping the Hill of Ruins. It is a memorial to the over ten-thousand civilians who were killed there during air-raids.

Now the city is rebuilt and again a proud and prosperous place. Its population is almost one million. It has become quite an international community where many languages can be heard and where many racial groups have found a new home.

Modern factories—Mercedes-Benz, Merck, Bayer, Robert Bosch—as well as breweries are in full production. The ancient mineral springs once again invite guests to warm pools, spas, and drinking fountains. Sports, libraries, museums, concert halls and theaters—including the two beautiful Royal Operas surrounded by parks and fountains as well as copies of ancient Greek statues—invite visitors to enjoy cultural events.

The police band still plays every Saturday and Sunday afternoon in the pavilion on the Castle Square. When our family in years past listened to the red-cheeked, earnest policemen playing march music, we girls fed the pigeons while our parents rested on one of the many benches shaded by majestic old chestnut trees. The brilliant flower-beds surrounding the pavilion as well as the two fountains and the tall Victory Column were always perfectly weeded and tended to.

I am thankful for the city father's decision to rebuild the destroyed historic buildings to reflect their past glory. Only the once Gothic City Hall, which stands in the background of the big market square, has a modern facade. It does not seem to belong there.

A tunnel was built under the market square to serve as an air-raid shelter during the war. After the war, the shelter was expanded into a first-class hotel. For many years this Bunker Hotel was the only place for travelers to stay overnight.

In its thousand-year history, Stuttgart has experienced many ups and downs. I hope that it will never be destroyed again. I still love my beautiful hometown in the valley.

Bell Stories

European church bells go back many centuries and serve many different purposes. Before the inventions of electricity and radio, church bells were rung to spread news of enemy attacks, fires, floods, and other catastrophes. They also announced happy occasions such as royal weddings, births, or the beginning of holy days.

The big cathedrals have several sizes of bells in their towers. The larger the bell, the lower its sound. These bells are fastened to sturdy ropes. It was the bell ringer's job to pull the ropes every hour to tell the time and make public announcements. Today, the bells are rung electronically.

Two of my favorite stories about bells are deeply embedded in my childhood memories. One concerns royalty, the other a young boy's guilt feelings.

The Silver Bell

Long ago kings and queens ruled the fertile valley of my hometown, Stuttgart, Germany. The city and valley were surrounded by dense woods. This forest was home to many wild animals including deer, rabbits, wild boar and bear.

Every autumn a Great Hunt was arranged for the pleasure of the royal family and its entourage. Hunters carrying bows and arrows and young knights blowing their horns were all part of this colorful party.

It was a lusty, happy event for all participants, young and old. All uninvited citizens were aware of the Day of the Royal Hunt and knew to stay away from the forest, as was the law.

In the meantime, servants cleared an area of the forest. This was where the Hunt Feast was to take place. Some men had dug a large fire pit and filled it with branches to be lit later for the roasting of wild game. Some maids were baking bread, and young servant boys carried kegs of wine in preparation for the celebration. When the meat of the boar or deer was prepared, it was roasted on a spit over the fire. The youngest servant boy's job was to slowly turn the spit until the meat was ready to eat.

Through the smoke of the wood fire and the delicious scent of roasting meat, one could observe the members of the hunting party arriving one by one. Tired and hungry they jumped off their horses and settled themselves on blankets placed on the forest floor. Now it was time to indulge in a wonderful feast of meat, bread, and wine.

On this cool, dark autumn night the light of the burning fire was sufficient to warm and brighten the air around. Soon the forest echoed with happy hunting songs and laughter.

No one noticed that a young princess named Kunigunde was missing. This was the princess's first hunt. She had been quite charmed by a handsome young knight who carried her bow and arrow. She looked lovely in her green hunting outfit with gold trim, and her favorite horse, Phillip, safely carried her through the thicket and brush during the hunt. This splendid animal had been her faithful companion since early childhood.

Kunigunde heard and saw the festivities of the hunting party, but she did not wish to participate. She just wanted to ride on with the young, handsome knight. He was equally well dressed for the occasion in a short red tunic over a longsleeved white shirt. Black tights and buckled shoes completed his costume. His cheeks were flushed red with excitement of the hunt and his long blond hair blew in the evening wind while he galloped alongside the princess.

The two young riders soon found themselves deep in the wilderness. The path ended near the narrow creek where their horses stopped for a refreshing drink of cool, clear water. The sun had set, and suddenly they realized that they were lost on this dark, cloudy night with neither moon nor stars showing the direction home.

The princess became frightened. She was near tears when her companion called out: "Listen, do you hear this? It is not a hunter's horn. This is the sound of a bell."

Kunigunde was relieved. "Yes, this is the bell from the castle chapel. Quickly, let's follow its sound before the ringing stops."

Soon they found the path they had taken earlier and were on their way out of the forest. The bell had struck midnight, calling the lost ones home.

"Thank God and all the saints for the safe return of our beloved daughter," the king called out. "I decree that a silver bell be poured by our finest silversmith. This bell will be hung up high in the cathedral's tower. It will ring every hour during the night. It will guide lost men, women, and children back to the safety of their homes."

After centuries, the little Silver Bell cracked and can now be seen in the castle's museum, where it rests among royal jewels, ancient armor, and weapons. It used to bring joy and comfort to all who heard it.

Karl and the Bell

It was a sunny spring Sunday morning, much to the delight of children and adults. Karl, a young boy full of spunk, was not much of a pious church goer. He was always late for services. His family looked forward to worshipping in their Sunday best. Father wore his black suit and top hat. Mother looked pretty in her blue Sunday dress, hat, and gloves. His sister was cheerfully wearing her frilly pink frock and black leather shoes. Together they walked out of their house into the warm sunshine in order to be on time for the worship service.

The bells were ringing. First the small ones with their friendly, lighthearted sound, then the tenors joined in and finally the large bells in heavy, low bass tones completed the call to worship. No one could have possibly overslept.

But Karl was not among the churchgoers. He had climbed over the back fence. He whistled a merry tune, ran here and there through the dew-fresh green meadows, and tried to catch butterflies. Karl pretended not to hear the church bells' call, "Come to church, come to church."

Tired after running through the fields and along a path, he rested on a moss-covered boulder. To his surprise he kept hearing the largest bell's call, "Come to church, come to church." The boy tried to ignore what he heard, but the sound of the bell became louder and more persistent. Karl jumped off the rock and turned around to see where this voice came from. To his horror he saw that the huge bell had come off the tower and was now chasing him—getting closer and closer. He raced to flee from the threatening call, "Come to church or God will punish you."

Karl felt his heart beat in his throat, and his heartbeat joined the rhythm of the bell, loud and clear. "Go to church or God will punish you."

The boy finally reached the safety of the sanctuary. Frightened and out of breath, he entered and sat down in the last pew. He felt like an outcast, and all alone.

The bell stopped haunting him. Peace gradually returned

to his tortured heart. The congregation recited the Lord's prayer, and Karl humbly joined in. ". . . and forgive us our sins." Karl felt that God had forgiven him. He was never late for church services again.

The Leonhard family, 1932. Children from left to right: Grudrun, age three; Christa, age 1; Siglinde, age five. Mother, Lydia; father, Karl.

Our Playground in the Forest of Stuttgart

We lived only a few minutes from the forest that crowned the hillside surrounding my beloved hometown. Everyone I knew loved to hike through it or take leisurely Sunday afternoon strolls along its well kept paths. Benches here and there invited mothers to rest while they watched their young children at play in the fallen leaves or as the little ones built tiny houses out of sticks or pine cones. Covered wooden shelters protected us during rain showers. No matter what the weather, playing in the woods was our favorite pastime.

When we were very young our nursemaid, Ellie, took her basket of mending along. When going to the forest, we first had to agree on which part of the woods we wanted to visit. Each area had its special attraction.

One day we chose the little stream full of smooth, gray rocks. We splashed barefoot in the clear water and built a dam across, using the biggest rocks we could find. Another day we worked on the cave we had started to dig the week before. Sometimes we played hide-and-seek behind the old oak and beech trees.

Wherever we stopped to play, we made sure it was near a bench so Ellie could do the mending. When we girls tired of running and playing, we joined her and she would tell us stories.

As we grew older we were allowed to go to the forest by ourselves and we often met other children. Yes, we all loved our forest—sturdy, protective, and ever predictable in its seasonal changes.

In March the anemones, the first wild flowers of spring, burst into bloom overnight. They transformed the forest floor into a carpet of white stars, a glorious reflection of the night sky above.

Before the ancient beech and oak trees would clothe their large, far reaching branches in new pale green leaves, the pink and white blossoms of wild cherry and plum trees, like bits of sun-bleached lace, peeked here and there between the gnarled, brown trunks of other deciduous trees.

April was the month when the Cuckoo could be heard. This bird does not hatch its own young. It lays its eggs in other birds' nests and lets them do the parenting while the Cuckoo's happy-go-lucky call can be heard day and night. It stays only a few weeks and then it is gone.

These birds are quite large, about the size of a crow, and light gray in color. As soon as we heard the first "cuckoo, cuckoo" we quickly ran to the place we thought the sound came from. But when we reached that tree, we heard the Cuckoo's call coming from an other direction. We held tight to our penny purses during these days of happy hunting, for the story says that if you actually see a Cuckoo while jiggling your coins, your purse will never be empty. However, in all the years we played that game, we never once saw a Cuckoo bird.

In May, the lily-of-the-valley flowers sent their lovely sweet fragrance across the forest floor. We picked big bouquets of them to take home or to give to our teachers. Father's birthday was in May and he always had a large vase full of these lovely May flowers on his birthday table.

Glorious summer brought young lovers to the forest for a special celebration. Each year they would carve their initials and the date into the smooth bark of "their" beech tree, promising eternal love for one another. Oh yes, these truly were "the days of wine and roses."

The carefree summer ended when the days grew shorter, the nights cooler, and the green leaves turned to crimson, orange and yellow. When we picked the last blackberries from the thorny bushes, the vines clung to our sweaters as if begging, "Please take our luscious sweet berries before they drop to the ground." We picked baskets full and happily ate them for supper soaked in fresh cream and dusted with powdered sugar.

Autumn was also the time when, after a night's cool rain, myriads of mushrooms popped out of the leaf-covered soil. Now it was time to meet with the "Nature Man" on weekends. He was a kind old soul with long white hair. We could not picture him to have ever been young. Year after year he lectured the young about the importance of and our responsibility to our environment. We met him at one of the big trees in the woods where he pointed his gnarled cane at a tree and explained, "Trees are the lungs of the cities. They provide us with oxygen while absorbing carbon dioxide. That is why we take such good care of our parks and forests. Whenever a tree has to be felled, a new one is planted immediately." We listened to every word he said. We knew he was right.

The Nature Man was also an expert on wild edible plants and mushrooms. He practically saved our lives after the war when food was extremely scarce. He introduced us to wild spinach, nettles, and dandelion leaves. Mother cooked the wild spinach and nettles, and we used the dandelions in our green salads.

The Nature Man also helped us identify mushrooms. It is a well known fact that for each edible one there exists a poisonous twin.

We picked whatever varieties we could find, but we kept only the ones that were safe to eat. Some of them were small and round, some were funnel shaped, yellow with thin stems.

Occasionally, we were lucky and came across one of the treasured Stone Mushrooms with its fleshy white stem and round, dark brown hat. What a delicious meal all these mushrooms made, especially when they were sauteed in butter with onions.

We also knew a "Nature Woman." We never spoke to her, and where she lived nobody knew. We only watched her strolling through the woods on paths leading from the city to surrounding villages and small towns. These trails were the ancient highways of our ancestors. The lady I speak of always wore a light gray pant suit (at a time when no woman wore slacks). She had silvery, shoulder length hair and wore sandals without stockings even in winter. She always had a smile on her sun tanned face. Her gait was light and bouncy, like that of a real "Earth-Angel." Someone told us she was a poetess, very exotic, and "other-worldly"; only the wings were missing.

Another dear person was part of our childhood. We saw her one day sitting on one of our favorite forest benches with her neighbor's fox terrier. She told us about her life and we found her fascinating. Her name was Miss Oettle. She lived in the old part of town, but took daily walks up the hill to the woods for exercise and fresh air. The dog was great fun because he always fetched the sticks we threw for him. Miss Oettle was probably in her seventies, a spry little lady, her hair pulled back in a small bun, her hands speaking of a life of hard work.

The following is one story I shall never forget. Miss Oettle was a seamstress for Queen Charlotte, the wife of the last king of Wuerttemberg.

Stuttgart is the capital of this German state. Until the end of World War I the many castles and palaces were occupied by royal families and their large households. After that war, in 1918, the monarchy was dissolved.

According to Miss Oettle, Queen Charlotte was a vain woman who, even during war time, insisted on long, full dresses and yards of precious fabric used as "trains" attached to her garments. Miss Oettle was distraught at such wastefulness. So, one day as the queen strolled along the sandy path of the royal rose garden, Miss Oettle saw the new dress she had just finished sewing being dragged through the dust. Poor Miss Oettle was so angered by this, she purposely stepped on the train of the royal gown.

The queen turned around and shouted, "How dare you step on my dress!"

Miss Oettle curtseyed and simply answered, "Your majesty, in these days of war we all should be mindful of taking good care of precious fabrics and not waste anything."

Needless to say, Miss Oettle was dismissed from her position of royal seamstress, but—with a twinkle in her eyes—she finished her story with, "After this incident, I never saw the queen dragging the train of her dress again. She always carried it, draped over her left arm."

Salamanders

The top of Mother's organ was covered with a long, narrow cloth. It was a black silk runner embroidered on each short end with red and yellow flowers and finished with pretty silk fringe. In the middle of the cloth a brass lamp lighted Mother's music books. On each side of the lamp was placed a handblown black glass salamander vase, head turned up, mouth open. One showed specks of yellow on its back, the other sported red ones.

I had learned from my nature book how to distinguish male from female salamanders, namely by the color of their spots: Yellow for females, red for males.

On special occasions, like birthdays or Mother's afternoon coffees, the glass salamanders were taken to the kitchen, filled with water and fresh flowers, and used for decorations on the dining table.

They really looked pretty and I often wondered if I would

ever be lucky enough to see one of these splendid creatures in the wild.

Salamanders are amphibians like frogs, meaning their larvae have gills like fish, but the adults have developed lungs and breathe air. Salamanders look similar to lizards but are bigger and move rather sluggishly. They have a smooth skin and live in cool, damp or muddy areas. They behave differently from the little green and brown lizards living in our rock gardens that sun themselves on warm rocks and rush away to hide as soon as a person comes near.

One day, seven-year-old Christa, my younger sister, came breathlessly running into our children's room where I had just finished my homework.

"I have found a new, narrow trail in the woods and I want you to hurry up and come with me to explore where it leads to," she announced.

I quickly closed my notebook and off we went running up the slope to the forest we loved so well. Christa showed me the newly discovered trail. It was covered with fallen leaves. We gingerly skipped along until we came to the abrupt end of the path. Wooden steps led down to a creek bed—thirty-five steps to be exact. We held on to the slippery rail and arrived safely where the sparkling stream wound its way through the narrow valley. A wooden bridge with low rails spanned the water, and on the other side steps led to the woods above.

"It must have taken this little stream centuries to carve a way through the rocky ground," I remarked philosophically as we looked upstream. Old beech trees flanked the banks. Some of their thick, gnarled roots had been washed loose by spring floods. They dangled freely as if to search for solid ground to anchor themselves.

"Let's swing from that big root over there," Christa suggested, pointing to the heaviest root close by. Swinging from it would have been a lot of fun, but the bank of the creek was too soft and muddy. We had to give up reaching this tempting site.

We carefully walked to the center of the old bridge. Each

slippery board creaked under our feet.

As we looked downstream about twenty feet, we discovered that the creek was being funneled into a huge cement pipe, tall enough for us to walk through. It was like a dark, wet tunnel with no exit in sight.

"Let's explore the tunnel." Christa was enthusiastic, but I shook my head.

"You may go and I will watch you."

My sister jumped over the low rail of the bridge and waded toward the pipe. "Squash, squash."

"It is dark in here, but I see a big yellow ball way back in the tunnel. It is stuck there. I'll go and get it." Christa seemed to have neither fear nor common sense.

"No, no," I shouted. "Come back quickly. You may get stuck in the mud like that yellow ball and I would have to come after you and save you. No, this very moment turn around and come back."

To my surprise Christa followed my advice. She headed back out of the tunnel without the ball.

Suddenly, she pointed to the ground and shrieked. "Ooh, what is this black creature? Come quickly, it moves."

"Do not touch it, I will be right there," I shouted back.

I really did not want to step into that soft creek bed, but I knew that I had to see for myself if only to save my sister from that "black creature."

I took off my shoes and socks and waded down the stream to where Christa stood, a stick in her hand.

"Do not poke the thing, it may bite you." I wanted to protect my little sister.

I barely recognized the black creature. It was partially covered with mud. We splashed some water on it.

"Do you see the yellow spots on its back?" I gasped. "My goodness, it looks just like the pretty vases on Mother's organ. It must be a salamander."

"Look, there crawls a second one with red spots. Perhaps they are a pair." Christa added in astonishment.

We did not want to go any closer or touch them. We stood

still and watched them for a while. They moved very sluggishly.

"Let's go home now, we have done enough exploring for one day," I suggested.

We dangled our muddy feet from the bridge and splashed until they were clean and rosy again. We put on our socks and shoes and climbed up the thirty-five steps to the newly discovered path which led us out of the woods.

A few days later we returned. This time we knew the way. We were curious to find out if the salamanders were still in the same spot. We slowly walked along the creek until we reached the entrance to the tunnel.

"They are gone." I was disappointed, but felt relieved. I certainly did not want Christa to pick one up and carry it home. I would not have been surprised had she done just that. She loved animals.

But what was this? As we glanced into the tunnel entrance we saw the ground moving. To our delight we saw little baby salamanders emerging from the mud. They were tiny, perfectly shaped and black like their parents but without spots. They would develop later. They pushed and struggled to free themselves from the heavy mud.

"We must help them." We felt responsible for their survival. Their parents were nowhere in sight.

"You poor little things."

We cupped our hands and filled them with fresh creek water. We sprinkled the water on the tiny bodies until they were all clean. We counted eight baby salamanders.

"How will they know what to eat, how will they survive?" Christa was worried. "Their parents don't seem to care what happens to these babies."

I had to calm my little sister. "God taught them long before they were born where to find food and how to protect themselves from enemies and bad weather. This is called instinct."

Christa was satisfied.

When we arrived home we quickly told Mother about the exciting adventure. While Christa was still talking, I slipped away to the living-room and admired again the beautiful shiny black salamander vases on Mother's organ.

"In nature they certainly look different. And they even live in mud," I thought.

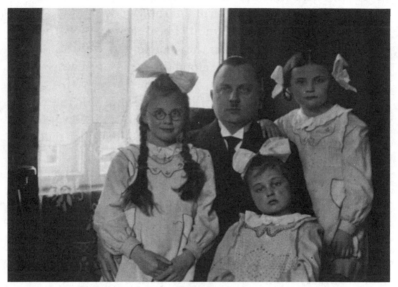

In our living room, 1936. From left to right: Siglinde, age nine; Christa, age five; Gudrun, age seven are pictured with their father.

Christmas and Other Traditions

Sunday of the Dead

The last Sunday in November is celebrated as the Sunday of
the Dead. It is a memorial day when all the graves are cleaned
of fallen leaves and other debris. After that chore is
accomplished, the graves are covered with fresh evergreen
branches and decorated with holly or blue spruce wreaths.
Occasionally a pillow or heart-shaped piece made of Icelandic
moss and pussy-willow branches can be seen on a child's grave.

Every church has a Tablet in Memory of Fallen Heroes.
On the tablet the names of brave soldiers who died in two World
Wars are engraved in gold. On this special Sunday, the Tablet is
draped with a veil of black cloth signifying mourning.

The weather is usually foggy, cold and rainy. Sometimes
flurries of early snow dance amidst the glistening raindrops.

We always visited the "Cemetery in the Woods" outside

Stuttgart, the "Waldfriedhof" (friedhof meaning court of peace; wald is woods). As a child I always had mixed feelings about going to this beautifully kept place on the Sunday of the Dead. In summer the mood was quite different. Tall rhododendrons were in full bloom among the green shade trees. The birds were twittering and all graves were ablaze with fresh flower arrangements which lasted through the summer months. It was like visiting a beautiful park. There were footpaths and benches, and we always took along some seeds and nuts to feed the squirrels and birds. They were tame enough to eat right out of our hands.

But in late November we were all bundled up in winter coats, caps and mittens. Oh, we still fed the little tame animals, but we talked in hushed voices, quietly walking alongside our parents. We paused here and there for a prayer in front of the grave of a friend Mother and Father used to know.

And the raindrops falling from trees, from gravestones and from our cheeks seemed like tears soaking the already damp soil beneath our rubber boots. But sometimes just before sunset, around half-past four in the afternoon, the clouds would move aside for just a short moment and sunbeams would ever so gently kiss our cheeks and warm our hearts, giving us hope for happiness and everlasting life.

Advent

I was always glad when the Sunday of the Dead was over and we could now look forward to the most wonderful time of year, Christmas.

Advent is the Latin word meaning "coming" or "expecting." Oh, yes, we were expecting the coming of the Christ child, the most precious gift of our Heavenly Father.

The four Sundays before Christmas, the Advent Sundays, were celebrated with a fresh green fir wreath on the dining room table. Four thick red candles decorated the wreath. The first candle was lit every evening during dinner of the first week. Two candles burned during the second week, three the third week, and four the last week before Christmas. While the candles were burning, we sang Christmas carols, read stories and memorized poems for the Christmas celebration.

The custom of the wreath goes back to ancient, pre-Christian times, when the winter solstice was celebrated by Germanic tribes. It was on the shortest, darkest day of the year, December 21, when men of importance were chosen to tie heavy dry fir branches around a wagon wheel. The wheel was then carried with great ceremony to the top of a sacred mountain. While chanting prayers to the sun goddess, the high priest lit the greens around the wheel with his torch. The fiery wheel was then sent down the hill, signifying the return of the sun towards Earth, promising longer days and warm seasons.

As a young adult I witnessed a similar custom in the Seven Hills along the Rhine river, near Bonn. There, the natives celebrated winter solstice by lighting huge bonfires on top of each of the Seven Hills. These fires burned all night to remind the citizens that the warmth of the sun would soon bring springtime and new life to the drab and colorless countryside.

Saturday evenings were very special during the Advent season. After supper we dressed up and waited for the arrival of neighborhood children we had invited for our Advent Hour. We greeted them at the door and handed each a spruce branch decorated with a candle in a clip-on holder. From the branch dangled a few chocolate wreaths covered with sprinkles of colored sugar. (After the celebration the children took these branches home.)

When everyone was assembled, the white candles were lit and the procession began. Mother played the organ and we sang carols while marching around the dining room table, single file, lead by Siglinde, the oldest in the group of children. All children watched their candles carefully and we never had an accident in all the years we did this.

After singing several Christmas songs, we blew out the candles and sat down. Now it was our family's turn to entertain our young friends. We recited our Christmas poems and played our wooden flutes. Sometimes our friends brought their instruments as well and we played together. What a lovely sound.

Afterward we rushed to the dining room, where Ellie, our maid, had prepared a beautiful table with platters of Lebkuchen, marzipan, and other sweets. The candles on the Advent wreath were lit and the electric lights dimmed. While we ate our snacks and drank hot chocolate, our friends told us about their special Advent traditions.

The first season we started this celebration after having just moved to Stuttgart, Helga and Gisela, who were also cousins, told us their story.

"Every Saturday night during Advent, the Advent Angel comes to our rooms while we are sleeping. The angel inspects everything and we make sure that all toys are put away, our clothes hung up and our slippers neatly put in front of our beds. The Advent Angel then quietly slips a little surprise in one of our slippers and disappears. Does the Advent Angel come to your house, too?"

We had never heard of this custom. Mother solved the puzzle by explaining. "Since we just moved here, perhaps the Advent Angel has not found out yet where we live. If you three sisters do as Helga and Gisela do, cleaning up your rooms, maybe—just maybe—the angel will get the message and will also put a little surprise in your slippers."

Miraculously, it happened. This custom stayed with us throughout our childhood.

St. Nicholas Day

According to history, Nicholas was a 6th century monk living in Turkey. He later became a bishop and saint. As a monk caring for the poor and needy, Nicholas is said to have left gifts of food on the doorsteps of the sick during the night. He did this labor of love secretly. For a long time no one knew who was the generous giver.

The birthday of St. Nicholas is December 6 and this day is celebrated differently depending where one lives in Germany.

A High Mass is celebrated in mostly Catholic areas like the Rhineland or Bavaria. Afterwards St. Nicholas, dressed as a bishop in all his glorious garments of white and gold, including a bishop's crown, rides through the town on a white horse. He is accompanied by Hans Muff, a servant who walks beside him and hands out sweets to the children along the way.

I grew up in mostly Protestant South Germany (Wuerttemberg). There Nicholas was dressed as a monk in a brown habit which was held together with a thick white rope around his waist. He had a long beard and carried a big sack with sweets for good children and switches for the bad. The switches were made of twigs, tied together with a ribbon. They were meant to be used by parents for spanking.

Nicholas appeared usually at night after all children were in bed. We girls carefully placed our polished shoes outside the door before quietly slipping under our bed covers in hopes that Nicholas would bring us goodies and not a switch. That would have been a terrible disgrace. It only happened once to a neighbor boy, Bernd. He received a switch because he had been mean to the family's maid, Maria. And sure enough Bernd got a good spanking from his dad for this misdeed.

We would have loved to have seen Nicholas in person, and one year this wish was granted. The doorbell rang loud and long that December 6. It was after dark. Who would come to see us this late and obviously uninvited? Mother answered the door and let the visitor in. It was Nicholas.

He was dressed in his brown outfit, just as we had seen it in pictures. He had a long beard and carried a big sack over his shoulder. We three sisters were afraid and hid under the dining room table. We did not expect to find this person we had so longed to see to be this intimidating. He had a loud, low voice and demanded that we come out of our hiding place.

"Now let us see who can recite the Lord's Prayer."

Oh, we had no problem with that. Neither did we hesitate when he asked us to recite the Christmas story exactly as it is written in the Bible.

Nicholas was pleased and we lost some of our fear. He

reached in his pocket and pulled out a tiny harmonica. He could play all Christmas carols on this little instrument and we sang along.

"Now, let me see if I can find something for you in my bag, but before I do I must be sure your names are written in my Golden Book. You probably know that my helpers watch you all year long and find out who is good or bad, and if you obey your parents and teachers."

He pulled out his Golden Book, put on his thick eye glasses and started to thumb through. Would he find our names there? Had we been good enough to have our names written in this book? Maybe not, maybe he would turn to his Black Book and find our names there. We felt like we were going to the Last Judgment.

"Ah, yes, here you are: Siglinde, Gudrun, and Christa. Yes, you have been good and industrious, learned your Bible verses and prayers and gave your teachers and parents no big heartaches. Now I will get you something from my bag."

With this, he turned around and reached for his sack which he had left in the corner of the room.

"Now if I had found your names in my Black Book, this is what would have happened to you. I would have taken you away, so that your parents could have some peace and joy."

He held up his bag. Two child-size, stocking-clad legs dangled from the sack. We screamed and again hid under the table. Too frightened to face Nicholas again, my sisters stayed in their safe place. I, however, felt brave enough to come out of hiding and receive some sweets for all of us.

We were so relieved when he finally left and never again asked for a personal visit from St. Nicholas.

The Christmas Market

"Daddy, Daddy, please take us to the Christmas Market. Today is the last day and Mother is busy with other things. Please, Daddy, take us just for an hour or so."

No loving father could resist little girls who pleaded this

earnestly and insistently with him. And so we bundled up and set out. We walked through snow and ice to the center of Stuttgart where, on the big square next to the Old Castle, the wonders of the Christmas Market were displayed.

Each booth was outlined with tiny electric lights, and the delectable scent of baking waffles and caramel almonds warmed our frozen noses. The center of the square housed the reason for the season, a huge papier maché cave housing the Holy Family, angels, shepherds with their sheep, ox and donkey, the three Wise Men with their camels and in the center of it all, the Christ child in the manger. The baby's golden halo filled the whole cave with glorious light. A smiling Mary and adoring Joseph stood by.

The snow laden spruce and pine trees surrounded the whole display and sheltered all figures from harsh winds and falling snow. It was a beautiful sight. Father directed us first to the manger scene. We listened to the children's choir and admired each figure of the display so lovingly repainted each year. After a while we got restless.

"Have you girls seen everything in the cave or do you need some more time?" Father asked.

"Oh yes, we are ready to visit the booths."

Father gave each of us a shining silver coin (about five dollars in value). "Spend it wisely," he told us with a smile. "You may buy anything your heart desires."

Little Christa headed right over to the nearest booth, which had items for her toy grocery store for sale. I remember her buying a scale, small triangular paper bags, some marzipan oranges and chocolate coffee beans.

Siglinde, the oldest, could not resist the book booth. She was the reader in the family and spent all her money on books. Among other stories she bought *Uncle Willie's Trip to Mars*. This book talked about the uncle's adventures with strange creatures and mountains made of cake and rock candy. Later Siglinde read the story to me, but when I came down with the mumps, she was kind enough to loan me this favorite book and I read it over and over again, admiring the pictures showing a strange and exciting world far away from Earth.

I stopped at the booth where doll furniture was being sold. I bought a little cradle painted blue with red hearts. It had a baby in it, and it fit perfectly in my doll house bedroom.

Father picked out a lovely hand carved angel ornament to take home to Mother. It was for our Christmas tree.

"Now, let us stop for some caramel almonds," Father suggested.

We were always ready for those. We had to stand in line for a few minutes until the shiny brass kettle containing sugar and almonds was ready to be emptied onto a tray. I watched the man in his white apron stirring the mixture. At just the right moment, the man turned off the gas flame and carefully poured the caramel colored contents onto the tray. There he separated the sugar coated almonds. After they had cooled off, he filled small bags for each of us and an extra one for Mother.

The fragrances of this and other sweets of the Christmas Market became inseparable memories which were important parts of our family's traditions belonging to the Christmas season.

Christmas Eve

"Softly the snowflakes are falling.
Quiet and frozen the pond.
Glistening the forest is waiting.
Rejoice, the Christ child soon comes."

This was my favorite carol that we sang as children around the piano or organ, "Rejoice, the Christ child soon comes."

The Christ child brings gifts on Christmas Eve. We girls always wrote letters to the Christ child a few weeks before Christmas. We asked for a gift or two. We never wanted to appear greedy. That way we always received surprise gifts besides the few we asked for. We put the letters on the outside windowsill in hopes that a gentle breeze would carry them to heaven where the Christ child would read them.

For weeks it seemed Mother locked herself in the veranda, a glassed-in sun-room next to the children's room. This room had become the Christmas workshop. "I have to help the dear Christ child to get everything ready," Mother explained.

But Christa and I—we shared the children's bedroom—wondered why we could never hear any talking come from this workshop.

"Surely, the Christ child and Mother would speak to each other while repairing our broken toys or sewing new doll dresses." Christa and I discussed this, but there was no answer. We never asked Mother about it either. It was all so mysterious and we liked it that way.

Our Christmas calendar helped us pass the seemingly endless weeks before Christmas Eve. Beginning with December, we opened a window every morning and admired the picture in it. We were always relieved when we could open the big door with the number twenty-four on it. It was the last to be opened and usually contained a lovely manger scene. The waiting was finally over.

The Christmas Room, Father's study, was kept locked for several days before Christmas Eve. This room had two doors, one from the hall and one from the living-room. It held all the secrets of the world. As hard as we children tried to steal a quick look when Mother unlocked one of the doors to enter, we never really could discover anything.

"Anyway, it would spoil everything for you," Mother told us. "The moment of surprise and delight would be gone."

She was right. One year on Christmas Eve we really saw the Christ child dressed in white with a gold wreath in his long hair. Or was it an angel? We did not dare to ask. This heavenly figure must have entered the Christmas room from the hall while we were singing carols in the living room. He slowly opened the door while ringing a bell. We watched in amazement. The whole Christmas room was lit by candles, the live tree as well. As we looked in awe, the Christ child disappeared.

Before we were allowed in the Christmas room, however, we had a tradition which was the same each year. Father always invited some head nurses from the hospital he was in charge of and, of course, his secretary. These were ladies with no families nearby and they enjoyed celebrating with us.

All dressed up, we welcomed our guests and invited them into the candle-lit living-room. When everyone was assembled, Father entered carrying the big family Bible, and we began singing carols accompanied by piano and organ. After that my sisters played a duet on the piano. Then I followed with a violin concert, accompanied by Mother.

Now we recited poems we had memorized, Father read the familiar Christmas story, and while we sang "Silent Night, Holy Night" the door slowly opened to the Christmas room and we were allowed in.

It was like entering a magic wonderland. We found our dolls in new dresses, the doll carriages with new pillows and blankets. My doll bedrooms, Siglinde's doll kitchen and Christa's grocery store were all freshly done up and filled with doll-sized goodies. (These last three playthings were only to be enjoyed during the Christmas holidays. Then they were packed away for the rest of the year.) New toys, books, and other gifts were there for us to open, and we gave our parents small gifts we had made for them.

After showing off our presents to each other and our guests, and after sampling some of Christa's marzipan fruits and vegetables from her store, we were called to the dining room for beautifully prepared platters of meats, cheeses, a variety of breads, deviled eggs, and potato salad.

It was the most beautiful night of the year.

Christmas Day

In the morning of Christmas Day all church bells rang in harmony and called everyone to worship. People who ordinarily would not attend church services would surely go twice a year— on Easter Day and on Christmas morning.

The glorious sound of the bells was followed by equally glorious organ music. The angelic voices of church choirs presenting the jubilant Christmas cantatas or the "Hallelujah" chorus by Handel gave this day a special meaning.

The rest of the day was spent with friends and family. December 26 is also a public holiday as are January 1 and 2.

Twelve Night

The third-graders are discussing the Christmas season. "What is the meaning of Twelve Nights?" The teacher asks.

In a chorus the children answer. "Twelve Nights is the holiday season between Christmas and Three Kings Day (Epiphany) on January 6. The following day we all go back to school."

"That is correct," agrees the teacher. "What do we celebrate on Christmas Eve?"

"It is the night when Christ was born in Bethlehem. Because God so loved the world and gave us His only son, Jesus, we give gifts of love to each other," the children answer.

Ingrid holds up her hands to add something. "Teacher, my parents grew up in a small town in Switzerland way up in the mountains. Children there receive gifts from their parents on January 6 to celebrate the gifts the Wise Men brought to the Christ child. Christmas Day is for church services only."

"How interesting. Does anyone else have a tradition to tell us about."

"Yes," Helga is anxious to tell the class about her relatives in America. "We have family members living in the USA. There Santa Claus comes down the chimney during the night of Christmas Eve. He quietly stuffs stockings and lays presents under the tree, and the children open these gifts on Christmas morning."

"Well," says Ellen, the smartest student, "we do not have fireplaces in Germany. There is no way that anyone could slide down a chimney to leave presents. He would end up in the furnace and would get badly burned." How clever she was. The class giggled.

"You see, there are many different ways to celebrate the

Christmas season. Now let us repeat the public holidays during Twelve Nights: Holy Evening, December 24; Christmas Day the 25; the second Christmas Day on the 26; New Year's Eve, called Sylvester, on December 31. New Year's has two days of celebration, and Three Kings' Day is on January 6."

On January 7 all students go back to school and all adults go back to work, the happy memories of Twelve Nights ringing in their hearts forever.

The Third Reich and World War II

The Third Reich

My earliest childhood memories go back to the time when we lived in Wuppertal-Elberfeld, a big industrial city in North-West Germany. The Wupper is a tributary of the Rhine river. The Rhineland, Ruhr area and Saarland had all been severed from Germany and annexed to France after World War I in 1918.

Elberfeld was in the process of rebuilding its industries in the 1930, but there was much unemployment, unrest, instability and confusion. Also the Communist Party had taken a foothold among the working classes.

It was 1932. My older sister Siglinde and I attended the private nursery school and kindergarten of Frau Gerda von Goetzen. She was a single lady and the daughter of a general. She ran a school for three to six-year-olds with great precision. I have many good memories of the time when I was a very young student at Tante Gerda's school.

Germany had many political parties during the early thirties. Socialists, Democrats, Zionists, and Communists among them. When Adolf Hitler became chancellor in January 1933, all former parties were outlawed. Hitler had established his own National Socialist German Worker's Party (NSDAP). But the Communists, now underground, struggled on against Hitler.

As a young child I had often heard the word "communist," but I did not understand the meaning of this strange sounding word. However, I have two very distinct memories connected to "communist."

The first one was when I had just come home from playing outside and had taken off my shoes in the kitchen as usual, I heard a loudspeaker announcing something. Our maid Frieda and I ran to the open living room window to listen and watch.

A policeman on horseback told us, by means of his bullhorn to immediately close shutters and windows and stay inside until further notice. We followed the instructions but peeped through the slats of the closed shutters. A few minutes later a group of men dressed in dark winter coats quietly walked past our house. They were guarded by armed policemen.

"These are Communists," whispered Frieda. "They are bad people and have to go to prison."

We watched until the men disappeared up the hill and around the corner. After a while we were allowed to open the windows again.

Later we heard that the police had expected a clash between the Communists and members of Hitler's party right on the street where we lived.

The second time I heard about Communists was on a day when six-year-old Siglinde decided to take her doll Walter for a walk in front of the house. She was allowed to go to the corner of the street by herself and then turn back. She had a beautiful doll carriage with lace pillows and a comforter. Walter wore a white shirt, purple short pants and a matching vest. Frieda had brought the carriage downstairs to the sidewalk and watched as my sister proudly strolled her doll.

Suddenly a group of boys about ten years old came running from a side street and attacked Siglinde. They pulled her braids, snatched Walter, and ran off with doll and carriage. Frieda heard my sister's screams. She ran after the boys and luckily wrestled the toys from these vicious youngsters. "These are Communists. They are poor and think they can steal anything from people who have something they want," Frieda explained.

Needless to say, this was the last time any of us were allowed outside without adult supervision. I had learned early in life to associate "Communists" with "bad people" and was really not surprised to learn later that Communists were accused of having burned down the Reichstag (Parliament Building) in Berlin.

In 1933 Father was transferred to Stuttgart to be a hospital director, and Mother was relieved. She did not like the atmosphere in big, dusty, industrial Elberfeld, neither did she enjoy the weather. It rained there almost daily.

Stuttgart is located in the South West of Germany, near the Black Forest. As the capital of the state of Wuettemberg, it was the seat of royalty for centuries. We enjoyed visiting the castles, rose garden parks with their lovely fountains, the Royal Opera and the concert hall. Everything was now open to the public since the last king abdicated after World War I.

And the city was clean! There were no smoke stacks spewing coal ashes, no bad Communists, no political demonstrations or street fights. The Stuttgarters were too sophisticated for such things!

We children learned the local dialect within weeks. Mother would have liked to hear us speak the beautiful High German which was spoken in Elberfeld.

My parents did not vote for Adolf Hitler in 1932. They were devoted to Paul von Hindenburg, the former president. His picture hung in our living room next to Adolf Hitler's. It was mandatory to have at least one photo of the new chancellor in every home.

We flew two different flags from our balcony: the old black, white, and red striped one and the new Third Reich flag with the swastika.

After a while I noticed that the old flag stayed rolled up in a corner. "This flag will not be flown anymore. It is outlawed." Mother explained.

Slowly, the power of the Third Reich crept into our everyday lives. It became quite noticeable that most men in our neighborhood wore the round pin of the NSDAP, Hitler's party. The women had joined the party's women's organization. The men paid their monthly dues and attended certain meetings. The women did much work with child care. They also made sure that mothers with more than three children had household help and six week's free vacation away from the family. The government built beautiful hotels high up in the Alps for these stressed mothers. Women with more than four children also received a letter of appreciation from Hitler, together with a Mother's Cross of Honor. The women proudly wore their crosses, especially on Mother's Day. Our minister's wife had born seven children. She received a gold cross pendant on a black-white-red ribbon. She often wore it.

The new regime did much to improve the workers' everyday lives. Conditions in factories were vastly improved and slums were torn down. Health care was brought to factories and schools. Twice a year everyone underwent a dental checkup. Physical exams as well as needed immunizations were administered for free.

Besides health care, Hitler also subsidized home ownership and car ownership. So the Volkswagen, the "Car of the People" was born. Large developments of single family homes outside cities replaced former slums. Workers now could enjoy their own homes in healthy surroundings. They could grow their gardens where they planted flowers and vegetables. Every year competitions were held among the workers' gardens, and prizes were given to the best kept ones.

Factories now had their own soccer teams, gymnastic groups and choirs. Industrial giants like Krupp Iron Works, Bosch, and Bayer built hospitals, maternity wards, and child care centers for their workers.

No wonder people were thankful and devoted to their new leader. He really seemed to care.

And while all these social improvements were made through the party, Hitler was able to take back those provinces that had been severed from Germany after World War I. We saw movies about the enthusiastic welcome the soldiers received from the local populations as they marched into the Saarland, Rhineland, Sudetenland, Austria, and other areas mostly along the East German border.

We gradually lost our personal freedom. The government had taken over most of our daily needs, had given people jobs, homes, cars, and health care. Education was excellent and mostly free through the university. After all this was accomplished, the population accepted new rules and laws willingly.

Suddenly, one morning all stores, offices, and other public buildings had signs on their doors saying, "The German Greeting is 'Heil Hitler.'" These signs must have been placed on Sunday, when every public building was closed. Come Monday morning we had to remember not to say "Good morning" or "auf Wiedersehen." No, it had to be "Heil Hitler."

How strange, especially for us children. However, we got used to it. We had no choice.

In school we had to line up every morning by the flag pole, raise our right arms and sing our national anthem, "Deutschland, Deutschland ueber alles." My arm got so tired. Luckily I was tall and stood in the last row of students resting my arm on the shoulder of the girl in front of me.

Our principal now wore the uniform of the SA, the brown shirts. The SA was organized as an instrument of physical training and political education of German men.

When I was ten years old, having passed the entry exam for high school (after four years of grade school), I was assigned to attend a former private all girls' school. This school was formerly owned by the Anthroprosophical Society. Like all private schools, it was confiscated by the government and became a public girl's high school. It was located along the hill side of

Stuttgart where many professionals had their villas.

The administration office, library, and teachers' lounge were located in the old mansion in the midst of a beautiful park. The janitor, Herr Leonhard, had a basement apartment in the mansion as well.

The school was a separate, very modern and well equipped building. I seemed to remember that the original owner had willed the property for the erection of this exclusive private school. It was once called Walddorfschule, but during the Third Reich it became Ludwig Uhland Oberschule in honor of a famous and much read local author of history.

Siglinde attended the Queen Katharine girls' high school and Christa went to the Queen Charlotte high school. Boys' high schools had a different curriculum from girls. During the nine years of high school boys concentrated mostly on math, science, chemistry, and physics. The gymnasium was a branch of high school emphasizing humanities such as philosophy, psychology, history, and foreign languages, including Latin and Greek, also biology. Girls studied more geography, languages, art, and music, but our majors were also like the boys': math, chemistry, physics, and history.

All schools taught religion as a subject. Girls learned "handiworks" (knitting, embroidering, crochet, sewing, cooking). English, French, and Latin were taught in all schools as well as all natural sciences. It was a varied and well rounded education. After nine years of high school and a very difficult exam (the maturum), the students who passed—and there were only a few—were ready to study their chosen field at a university. Most students took the exam after six years of high school, then branched out into specialized, career oriented schools. Every young person was well educated in any field, may it be technical, scientific, or social.

Hitler Youth

When one reached the age of ten, he or she was automatically enrolled in the Hitler Youth. We had to buy our uniforms and were told by mail where to meet. I had learned a lot from my older sister. She had been a "Jungmaedel" for two years before it was my turn to join.

My leader was sixteen-year-old, blonde, beautiful Rosel Zwink. I shall always remember her as an example of the ideal German woman.

The leaders of the ten to fourteen-year olds had to be first rate high school students, well trained in politics, sports, and music. Rosel taught our group of ten girls to march and sing. She also told us about the struggles of Adolf Hitler and his loyal comrades. Many of Hitler's followers were killed as they marched in Munich. The day of that massacre became a national holiday (November 9) and the men who died became national heroes.

Rosel instilled in us great respect and loyalty toward the Party and country. When we were in uniform we had to behave well, use good manners, and be helpful to older people. After air-raids we had to help clean up areas that had been damaged or destroyed, always wearing our uniforms. On Saturday afternoons we had sports in the gyms of a girls' high school.

But once a month during the summer we met in the forest to gather blackberry leaves. Afterward we delivered our bags of leaves to a tea company in Stuttgart. There, the leaves were spread out and dried. Later they were sold as German Black Tea. It made a wonderful caffeine free drink in place of the imported Indian or Chinese teas.

We were proud to do something for the German economy. In general we were encouraged to buy German products, especially fresh fruits and vegetables, and to stay away from out of season, imported goods.

Religion

By 1942 I felt an antireligious trend was appearing. We were still taught Christian religion in school. It was a subject like any other and we were given grades in Religious Instruction. A Lutheran minister taught Protestants, and a priest came once a week for the Catholic girls. No other religion was represented.

One day our home room teacher gave each of us a letter to take home. In it our parents were informed that they could chose to let their daughters remain in Religious Instruction or let them join a newly formed course called "Weltanschauung," Philosophy of Life. I noticed that all the girls whose parents were active in the Party joined this new group.

Father called my sisters and I into his study and, having read the letter, explained to us that his conscience would not allow him to let us take the new course. We hung our heads and left Father's study,

"I expected that. Father is so old-fashioned. I wish for once he would let us do something that's 'in.' We already know all those hymns and Bible stories. I wish I could find out what this new course is all about." I mumbled to myself. Siglinde and Christa agreed, but we quickly dropped the subject. Father had spoken and that was it.

And so we kept on taking Religion. We continued to learn the ancient Lutheran hymns—some had twelve verses—and Bible stories and Psalms. Way down inside my heart I knew that Father was right. But I was thirteen and yearned to be free to make my own decisions. "Not as long as you live in this house." Father's words still echo in my ears. More and more we became involved it disputes with our parents over religious matters.

I have no idea what was taught in the Philosophy of Life course. I never asked my friends and they did not share any of the teachings. After a while the Old Testament was stricken from the curriculum because it was labeled as a Jewish History Book. We occasionally saw people we did not know wearing yellow stars of David made from cloth with "Jude" (Jew) printed across them.

I remember well the first time I saw a lady wearing this sign on her coat. I was quite startled. I was wearing my uniform together with some other girls. We were on our way home from one of our Hitler Youth meetings. The lady came towards us, stopped in front of us and said, "We are proud to be Jews." We passed her quickly and quietly.

I do not remember if our leader, Rosel Zwink, ever discussed "The Jewish Problem." Maybe it came up once when we talked about Hitler's desire to purify the Arian race. Being blonde and blue-eyed was the ideal.

Siglinde symbolized this ideal as well; however, Christa and I had dark brown hair, tanned in summer, but, thank goodness, we had light colored eyes. From Mother's side we had inherited the dark hair, Father's ancestors were all blond. I envied Siglinde's Northern traits, but her skin also was very light and she had to suffer terrible sunburns—so did Father.

When the only synagogue in Stuttgart was burned during Kristall Nacht, I remember Mother telling us, "When a government causes religious shrines to be destroyed, the grace and blessings of God will not remain with such a country." I often thought about these words at the end of the war when everything ended in total collapse and ruin.

The Jewish population in Stuttgart was small. Many had already left for the USA. Father helped Dr. Jaeger escape before the borders were closed and no one could leave the country. Now it was time for Hitler to establish his own church, called the German Christians. This group never became very strong in Stuttgart. They met on Sundays in the chapel of the Old Castle in the center of the city. (The old Castle was more like a fortress, originally surrounded by a moat. That was centuries ago. Later the moat was filled in and the big cobble stone market square was built. The New Castle was created in classic Renaissance style, an elegant palace.)

Some of our neighbors joined the German Christians and the children told us that the German flag had replaced the crucifix and Hitler's book, *Mein Kampf* (*My Struggle*) had replaced the Bible. But I also learned that the congregation read from the book *Parcival*, which contains the story of the Holy Grail.

In the summer of 1944 the castle was destroyed together with the entire center of Stuttgart, everything went up in flames in an inferno that lasted for many days.

In the meantime the Lutheran Church went through some

drastic changes. In Wuppertal-Barmen a group of Lutheran theologians wrote a new confession. It became the Declaration of Barmen. I believe this to be the last Protestant Confession written.

This Lutheran group spoke out against the Party and government, went underground, and became the Confessing Church. Many of their clergy ended up in concentration camps, including the young theologian, Dieter Bonhoeffer. He died for his faith. Dr. Reinhold Niemoeller was spared this fate. He survived imprisonment, wrote about his experiences, and became very famous after the collapse of the Third Reich.

Biblical Names

Our butcher's daughter was Christa's age and they went to grade school together. Her name was Esther. Her brother's name was Fritz. We never knew Esther's middle name. In fact, nobody uses a middle name, not even an initial, except on official documents like passports and birth certificates.

Frau Seeger, our butcher's wife, helped out in the store. She always wore a clean white apron. We children loved to accompany Mother there because Frau Seeger always smiled and gave us a slice of bologna or other cold cut.

One day Frau Seeger was in tears as we entered the store. She told Mother that she had received a letter from the government telling her and her husband not to use their daughter's first name anymore because it was Jewish. They had to call her by her middle name, Brunhilde. We were shocked. It must have been 1943 by now. It was so strange not to call her Esther anymore.

My sister Siglinde's middle name is Ruth, mine is Marta, both Biblical names. Our youngest sister's name, Christa Ingeborg, was no problem. I noticed that some girls by the name Christa or Christina changed the spelling to Krista or Kristina, to make it seem less of a Christian name. Of course, Siglinde and Gudrun are names right out of the Norse Mythology and, therefore, highly regarded.

All men had to trace their ancestors back to the seventeenth century to prove they were Arians and had no Jewish blood in their veins. Luckily Father's family had lived in the same small town of Botenheim since the sixteen hundreds and it was easy to get the needed information from city hall and church records.

Next in question was the hospital's name. It was built by the Evangelical Association, a church which had founded many hospitals, orphanages, nursing homes, homes for retarded citizens, and kindergartens. Many of the nurses were parish nurses, hired by the small town governments.

Father was in charge of all the institutions in South Germany and Switzerland. The hospital in Stuttgart was named Bethesda, the Retired Nurses Home was then Tabor, both Biblical and, therefore, unacceptable. The hospital became Albrecht-Krankenhaus (after the founder of the Evangelical Association, Mr. Albrecht). Tabor was changed to Parkheim. Tabor was burned out in an air-raid, after all the retired nurses had been evacuated to Austria. The hospital, after suffering much damage during the war, once again became Bethesda after the demise of the Third Reich.

Churches were strictly observed. We were made aware that every Sunday during services spies were present to listen to the preaching. Our ministers had to be very careful not to say anything negative about the government. I was always relieved when our pastor prayed for our leaders and, of course, also for victory during the war. Our church was totally destroyed in 1943.

It is hard to believe that the Third Reich existed for only twelve years—six years of peace, followed by six of war. So much good came at the beginning, raising people's hopes for a united Germany that prospered and regained its national pride after the disaster of the lost first World War. Instead we had another lost war, eighteen million dead or crippled (one fourth of the total population), the country divided into four zones, occupied by former enemy troops, and East Germany made into a Communist Satellite State.

A No Man's Land between East and West Germany was established. In this five mile strip no one was allowed. All trees had been felled. The East German border yard could easily see East Germans trying to flee to the West by crossing this barbed-wire and landmine infested strip. Most of these refugees were shot to death as they fled.

Later, the Berlin Wall was erected. This wall not only divided the former capital, Berlin, but went along the border between East and West Germany through small villages and towns, often separating neighbor from neighbor.

West Germany was occupied in the North by the British military, near France by the French, and in the South by American troops. We were not allowed to travel between these zones without a permit issued by the occupying military governments.

This was our legacy. Our generation was left with guilt and shame and the hatred of the whole world. It took many years and several generations before Germany recovered from the Third Reich which had been promised by Hitler to be the Thousand Years of Peace.

It lasted twelve.

My father's family, 1920. From left to right: brother, Eugene; Mother, Gottliebin; sister, Frieda; my father, Karl; sister, Emma; father, Karl Leonhard.

My mother's family. From left to right: Marie Vincon Wintterle, Marta, Paul, Lydia (my mother), Ludwig Wintterle.

Where Have All the Soldiers Gone?

This popular song of the 1970s is still on my mind. I can easily identify with its message. At the beginning of the war all eighteen to forty-five-year-old men were called to arms. Many professionals were exempted. This included physicians, pastors, priests, actors, and men in leading positions. Those with any physical handicaps also were excused from serving in the military. My father was born with a clubfoot, a crippled left foot much smaller than the right. Thank God, he did not have to go to war.

I watched the men in our neighborhood. Some were older than forty-five, some had political careers. Most were members of the Party—the only political party allowed—namely the National Socialist German Workers' Party (NSDAP).

Gustav Kiefer was the only child of minister friends of my parents. His father had been killed in France during the devastating Battle of Verdun during World War I. His widowed mother wished for my parents to be her son's guardian in case she should die before he grew up. I very much wished for him to become my older brother. I was the middle of three sisters. We had no brother, so I felt deprived. But Gustav's mother lived a long life, so the young man remained just a good friend of the family.

When Gustav turned seventeen he was obliged to join the nonmilitary work force called Arbeitsdienst. These young men had to help out wherever an emergency arose. They carried spades instead of weapons. This service lasted for one year. After that they were ordered to become soldiers.

Gustav spent two Christmases with my family. The first time he wore the brown uniform of the work force. He was on furlough and came to see us. My sisters were both sick with the mumps and had to spend Christmas in bed. I relished the opportunity of sitting on his lap while he told us about his experiences helping to build the West Wall, a defense line between Germany and France.

Just before World War One the French built a similar fortification against the Germans. They called it the Maginot Line. The British called it the Siegfried Line. They made fun of this defense wall with its bunkers and trenches. The British soldiers sang a song about it which began, "We are hanging our washing on the Siegfried Line, on the Siegfried Line, ha, ha, ha . . ." They did not take the German armies seriously.

I remember Gustav's shiny boots and polished spade, and I loved the scent of his uniform, leather belt and shoulder strap. He laughingly told us, "The boots and spade do not always shine like this. After digging all day along the West Wall, they are covered with mud, but before we go to bed we have to clean and polish them to have them ready for the next day."

As I sat on Gustav's lap, I snuggled up against his shoulder. He looked so handsome. He was so full of life and humor. Oh yes, I would have loved to be his six years old little sister.

The second time Gustav visited us on Christmas was a few years later. He was now a strapping young officer and ready to go to war. The fighting had spread to the Soviet Union and

Communism had to be stopped.

This time none of us was sick. We sang Christmas songs together and when Father read the familiar story from the Family Bible, our youngest sister Christa wanted to sit on Gustav's lap.

We had a lovely Christmas celebration but we were haunted by the knowledge that Gustav had to leave for the Russian Front the next day. Would we ever see him again? Would he also be killed like so many of our friends? We tried not to think about it while waving good-bye when he left our home that night.

A few months later we received the news that Gustav had been wounded by enemy artillery. His right arm from the shoulder down was badly broken and mangled. He was recuperating in the Red Cross hospital in Stuttgart. Mother and I visited him and took him sweets and flowers. His arm was in a cast. A sling, fastened to the ceiling by a hook, kept his arm immobile. He had to stay like that for three months. I was so thankful that he did not lose his arm or get killed.

What I did notice was the blush of the pretty young nurse who took care of him. Thank God. Gustav did not have to go back to the Russian Front. His arm was permanently damaged.

After the war he married the pretty nurse. Our family attended the lovely wedding, and I was happy for Gustav.

Our plumber's son, Helmut Mayer, was not so lucky. On his eighteenth birthday he was called to arms, and soon after we saw his obituary in the newspaper.

It read, "Our son Helmut died for his country's glory and victory. He was our only child. His promising life ended on the steppes of Russia. We are in proud sorrow. His mourning parents, Mr. and Mrs. Emil Mayer."

What a heartbreak. "In proud sorrow"? How could that be? I knew that our government, and all governments of the world, told bereaved parents of the "honor and glory" of having their sons killed on a battlefield far away from home.

"Our leaders make war and our children have to die," was Father's sad comment. He was right.

Helmut's dear mother never recovered from her loss. She

had a nervous breakdown and had to spend the rest of her life in an institution.

When the phone rang one day and a relative of Father's spoke, I had an uneasy feeling. I had answered the call and heard a distraught voice saying, "I just want to tell you that your cousin Helmut Stengel was badly wounded. I could no longer listen, so I called Mother. When Mother started to cry on the phone I knew Helmut was dead. We all cried. Helmut was the elder son and was expected to take over his parents' farm while his brother Walter had plans to study theology. Now all plans had to be changed. Walter later took over the farm.

Millions of our best young men lost their lives in that vast country, Russia. Their bodies were never returned to Germany. Maybe they lie somewhere buried in Russian soil, only God knows where. The longer the war went on, the younger and older the soldiers became. Near the end, all sixteen to sixty-five-year olds were called to the Volkssturm. These men were barely trained to handle weapons but were expected to save house and home from the intruding enemy armies who were already at Germany's borders. On our fronts—East, West, and South—the enemy stood poised and ready to overrun our country.

The Volkssturm wore no uniforms, only armbands. They were given a few hand grenades or lightweight machine guns. With these pathetically inadequate weapons our men were expected to defend our homeland against tanks, bombs, and artillery. How sad!

Herr Lohr across the street was "missing in Stalingrad" along with hundreds of thousands of others. These "missing" soldiers were never found. The Battle of Stalingrad was the turning point in World War II. A million men died there. After Stalingrad fell back into Russian hands during a bitter cold winter, the German troops steadily retreated, just like Napoleon's troops a century earlier. The Russian winter had again proved to be the victor.

Herr Ladewig and his family lived in the flat above ours. He was a pianist and voice teacher, who was captured in Russia and kept in a prisoner of war camp. He was finally released in

May 1950, five years after the war ended. The Russians did not want to let him go because they needed him to entertain the Russian officers in their clubs. At least he had better treatment than his comrades who had to walk home from Siberia. It took many months for them to cross thousands of miles, their frozen feet wrapped in rags, their uniforms dirty and torn. Many lost toes, fingers, or noses during the bitter cold and merciless winter months.

Another generation of brave and patriotic German soldiers was sacrificed in the second lost world war in twenty-five years.

> ". . . Where have all the soldiers gone?
> To the graveyards, everyone.
> Oh, when will they ever learn,
> Oh, when will they ever learn . . ."

Gudrun Martha Leonhard, eleven years old, winter 1940.

A Child's Prayer Answered

We loved our beautiful, bright yellow canary, Hansel. He was a Christmas gift well before World War II and lived with us through the worst of the war. He chatted to his image in the cage's mirror, and warbled his sweet tunes when we all sang around the piano. But he sang the loudest when we three girls had disagreements and argued. The more we raised our voices the louder he sang, his little throat swelling like a tiny powder puff. He only sang while in his cage. When we let him fly around the living room, he always landed on the highest spot in the room, which was the gilded frame of an oil painting which Opa Wintterle had completed as a young man (Opa Wintterle was Mother's dad).

Hansel felt safe up there, and I can still hear him scolding us from his high perch. His scolding voice was quite different and not as sweet as his singing. The best way to get him back into the cage was to lure him with special treats, like a piece of bird-biscuit or bits of salad greens.

In the fall of 1944, all schools were closed because of the danger of air-raids. Stuttgart had suffered much damage inflicted by Allied bombs. Children were evacuated in 1943. They had to live and go to school in small country towns or live with relatives. Christa and I moved in with Oma Wintterle in Heilbronn. But after the invasion of the Allied Forces in Northern France our parents insisted we return to Stuttgart. We were now taught by private tutors. We could already feel the vibration of exploding bombs and artillery, like constant, distant thunder. The front was coming closer every day.

"From now on we will stay together to the end," Father had decided.

In spite of constant danger, our lives had to go on. This included standing in line for food and running to the shelter when bombs threatened. My main concern was the lack of food for our beloved Hansel. We had subsidized his diet with bits of bread and nuts, slices of apples and their seeds, but in order to stay healthy we had to come by regular canary food. Most of the stores were burned out, boarded up or empty. Only one store, The Pfitzer Seed Co. in the ruins of the center of town, sold small bags of bird seed to its good customers. The secret was owning one of their paper bags, stamped with the name of the company. I do not know when they started this procedure. I did own one of these used bags, but mine was not stamped. To get more bird food, one had to bring to the store an old bag which was then filled with a two month supply. It was so complicated!

When I woke up one cold and rainy November morning, I went immediately to Hansel's cage to feed him. But his box of seeds was empty.

"Mother, today I will try to get some food for Hansel. He has nothing left to eat. I have saved the paper bag from last time I bought his seeds from the Pfitzer Company. I absolutely will not come back empty handed. I will not let our poor bird starve. Today is ideal weather.

It is foggy and rainy and it is quite safe. Hopefully no enemy planes will come and shoot at people standing in line."

Mother had faith in me and sadly let me go.

We always said a prayer before leaving home, so I prayed while Mother listened, "Lord, go with me each step of the way, and bring me home safely. Oh God, I pray."

I folded my little, unstamped paper bag, stuck it in the pocket of my blue rain coat, kissed Mother good-bye and ran down our hilly street. It was almost eight o'clock and the store would open at nine. I knew a long line of customers would already be forming outside the store. I prayed all the way, "Oh, God, please let me get some food for Hansel."

I passed the hospital and noticed that the windows in Father's office were open. That was always the first thing he did after getting to work.

The street was full of people with open umbrellas. They all had to get to work on foot. The streetcars had ceased to run and only a few private citizens were allotted rations for gasoline.

I finally made it through the rubble and ruins and stood in line until nine o'clock. The store was opened and I was constantly pushed forward by the crowd behind me. I finally reached the entrance. "Oh, God, please let the lady accept my unstamped bag." I prayed. The clerk in her white coat reached for my bag and started to fill it.

Then, suddenly, she turned around and simply said, "I cannot fill your bag. If you were one of our good customers you would have the proper stamp that is required. Sorry."

She handed me the empty bag and helped the next customer. I was devastated. I had stood in the rain and cold for two hours, all in vain. I had prayed fervently and God had ignored my sincere request. What a disappointment. My head was spinning. I left the store in a daze. What now? I could not go home empty handed. Suddenly a gust of wind blew into my face. It had stopped raining. I looked down onto the sidewalk. Some fallen leaves and paper had blown right to my feet. I picked up the damp paper. It was a Pfitzer Seed Company bag. And, yes, it was stamped.

I quickly stood in line again. "Weren't you here a while

ago?" The clerk asked. "I don't know where you got the stamped bag, but you will now get your canary food."

I thanked her, paid, and quickly left the store.

I was so elated and relieved, I could hardly breathe. I could not wait to show my family the full bag. When I passed the hospital on my way home, Father's French windows were closed. But that did not deter me.

"Vati, Vati, look," I shouted.

Father opened his window and waved.

"Look, I got the bird food," I shouted excitedly as I showed him the bag.

"That's wonderful," Father smiled. Then he closed the window.

He was probably in the middle of an important meeting. How nice of him to answer my call.

Thank you, God, for hearing my prayer and sending me that stamped bag. To me, this was a true miracle.

The Letter

Our postman always rings twice. It is the law. He is the letter carrier, bringer of good and bad news. We did not see him often because he always rang the doorbell after delivering the mail to the letter box inside the entrance hall. Once a month, however, he came to the door to collect the two marks ($1.00) radio fee.

I never knew how the post office was notified that we had a radio. Much later I asked Mother about it She explained. "It is our duty to let the post office know when we purchase a radio. Nowadays we also have to tell them about owning a television set. There is a combined fee, and it is still collected by the postman at the beginning of each month."

The gas man also came every month. He read the meter and we paid him cash. He was an older man who carried a heavy address book and wore a blue uniform. The gas meter hung inside, next to the kitchen. I often held the ladder for him as he climbed it, read the meter, and noted the amount of gas we had used. After paying him, Mother always had to sign his big address book.

The postman and the gas man carried a lot of cash, but no one would have ever thought of robbing these faithful public servants.

We were all excited the day we received a letter from Aunt Marta, Mother's sister. She was married to Uncle Albert, a psychiatrist. They lived in far away Goerlitz, Silesia, an area close to the Polish-German border. There, Uncle Albert had taken a position in the psychiatric hospital.

I was Aunt Marta's godchild, bearing Marta as my middle name. Every birthday I received a package from her with the most wonderful and unusual gifts. One year it was a big box of everything I needed to play post office, namely play envelopes, writing paper, postcards, stamps, a letter scale, play money, and even rubber typesetting letters and an ink pad so we could print our own greeting cards.

My sisters, Siglinde and Christa, were as delighted as I. We spent many happy afternoons playing post office. I was always the post mistress, my sisters, and friends were the customers.

"We have almost used up all our supplies, let's make some more ourselves," I suggested. "Siglinde, you cut out squares for envelopes and fold three corners to the middle. Then you can glue a sticker where the three points meet and you have an open envelope, you see?"

Mother donated some scraps of colorful wallpaper we could use for cards and writing paper, and Christa and I were busy measuring and cutting. Now we were ready to continue our game of post office.

Aunt Marta and Uncle Albert had lost their only child, a baby boy, at birth and so my sisters and I became their "substitute children."

Mother sent photos and some of our artwork to them regularly. In that way they could participate in our progress and development over the years.

As I grew older, Aunt Marta would write and tell me of her

life as the wife of a psychiatrist. She took patients for walks in the hospital's park, sat with them on a park bench and listened to their stories. She even gave them art lessons and some of their paintings hung in Uncle Albert's office. She often entertained lavishly using her fine china, silver, and crystal, and she wore long party dresses for special occasions. I thought she lived like royalty.

The important letter that had just arrived at our house was addressed to Mother only. And Mother closed the door behind her when she went to the living room to read it. We knew that she wanted to read her sister's note without being interrupted.

It was the spring of 1943. The war was getting more intense. The fighting had spread to the Soviet Union in the East and General Rommel's Africa Corps was engaged in the desert of North Africa. Uncle Albert was called to serve in a Red Cross hospital on the Russian front. Now Aunt Marta was all alone, far away from the rest of her family members who were living in the Western part of Germany.

"I wonder what Aunt Marta is writing Mother about," I thought. "I hope it is not bad news from Uncle Albert, or did she have another still born baby?" I was concerned about her.

As I stood and listened at the closed living room door, I heard sobbing. The letter must have contained some serious news. I could not wait any longer, I had to know.

I carefully opened the door. Sunshine was streaming through the high French door windows and gently touched Mother's brown hair. She sat in her favorite armchair, the letter in one hand and the other hand holding her white handkerchief and wiping her eyes. I entered the room.

Mother was too upset to speak. She quietly handed me the letter and I read what it said .

My dear Lydia,
I am in a terrible dilemma. There is a new law in the land.
Every woman whose husband is in the military and who has
no children under sixteen years of age to care for is obliged to
go to work in the munitions factory near by. As you know I

*have never worked outside the home and never expected to do
anything but occasional charity work or helping Albert with
his patients, which I thoroughly enjoy. I find it humiliating for
a doctor's wife to become a factory worker. The pain of having
no child to care for and no husband home is only multiplied
by this order.*

*Please, help me. You have three healthy daughters and I
know you love them dearly. I am asking, yes begging you, to
send one of them to live with me. Gudrun, my godchild would
be my first choice. She could go to school here and I could
shower all my love on her. By sending your thirteen-year-old,
you would give my life new meaning and happiness.*

*Of course, this arrangement would only last until the war's
end and everything would go back to normal.*

*I worry about Albert. He is not well and yet has to serve
on the Russian front. And winter is near. We all know how
deadly cold the Russian winters are.*

*Please, Lydia, pray for us. I am looking forward to your
positive answer.*

*I am your loving sister,
Marta.*

I was as stunned as Mother. I gave her back the letter. She
quietly folded it and put it back into the envelope.

"What are you going to do? Are you sending me to Goerlitz?
Is Aunt Marta's happiness really up to me?" I had so many
questions, but Mother just shook her head.

I left the room. I certainly did not want to be chosen to
leave my family and travel to the East, seven hundred miles
closer to the Russian front. That letter could have changed my
life, but it was never mentioned again.

Aunt Marta did go to work in the munitions factory for a
while. The German troops pulled back from the Soviet Union
more and more. The battle for Stalingrad was lost. It was the
worst slaughter of the whole war. Over one million men, friend
and foe, died in the ruins of this Russian city.

As the German troops retreated, hundreds of thousands of refugees went with them. Many of them were White Russians from the Ukraine who were Pro-German during the war. They feared for their lives in face of the possibility of the Red Army overrunning their land and killing everyone who had sided with the Germans.

And I was supposed to go and live near that chaos? It was hard for me to understand Aunt Marta's request.

A few months later, Uncle Albert was released from the military. He had contracted tuberculosis and was sent to a sanatorium. While he recovered there, the psychiatric hospital where he had worked before the war was closed and the patients relocated to the West. As soon as Uncle Albert was released from the sanatorium, Aunt and Uncle sent all their goods to Oma Wintterle in Heilbronn. Christa and I were still living with Oma, away from the air-raids in Stuttgart.

Everything was stored in Oma's house. I remember seeing the baby carriage that had never held a child, but was full of preserved jams and pickles. Many of the jars were broken during transport by train. Much of the beautiful furniture that Aunt Marta had treasured was scratched or broken. I cried when I saw how her life had been devastated. Aunt and Uncle were now refugees along with hundreds of thousands who had fled the threatening Russian front. With broken hearts they left the little grave of their baby behind never to return. After the war, Silesia became a part of Poland and all Germans were displaced.

I often wondered what might have happened if I had been sent there. I might not have survived the chaos of the war's end.

British bomber shot down by German flak during an air raid on Stuttgart. It landed in the forest behind our house. The pilot was killed.

The Dud

We did not know whether it was a time bomb or a dud.

A time bomb could hit the ground and make a crater but not explode for up to two weeks. We had encountered these bombs many times and heard explosions long after air raids. Often while playing in the forest we heard bombs going off nearby or in the distance. BOOM!

Duds were different. They did not have timing devices built in; they simply did not explode.

During the summer of 1944. The invasion by Allied troops in Northern France was in full swing. Saturation bombing of all major German cities had to be endured by the civilian population. Trains were attacked by dive bombers including the British Spitfires.

During the day we would see and hear masses of Flying Fortresses. They flew so high that no German fighter planes or artillery could reach them. We saw these tiny silver specks of bombers glistening in the sunlight, we heard their droning, and felt the vibration of hundreds of engines. Was their goal our city? Or would they fly on perhaps to Munich? We stood and waited. Death and destruction were always near but unpredictable.

Air raids during moonlit nights were especially haunting. Our city was pitch black, invisible to enemy planes. The full golden moon rising behind trees created shadows of their waving branches. These branches seemed like long, gnarled fingers, eerily reaching out to grab us and sling us up and away, from "here to eternity."

This was such a night. The sirens had chased us out of our warm beds. I always slept in a jogging suit then and wore my wrist watch day and night. My most treasured possession, my violin, was placed next to my bed. I slipped on my shoes, clutched the violin case and ran with my family to the tunnel-shelter in the hillside.

Suddenly, as we were still some four hundred feet from the shelter, the night sky was brightly lit by hundreds of flares on little parachutes floating towards the ground. The flares helped us find our way. We would never have dared to use a flashlight for fear it would give our city away to the enemy.

The flares looked pretty hanging in the black night sky. They had been dropped by smaller enemy planes to mark the territory to be bombed. They formed a huge square right above us. We knew that the following bombs were meant for us.

While running to the shelter we smelled the chemicals used in the artificial fog produced to disguise the location of our city. But it was too late. Shivering with cold and fear we arrived out of breath at the hillside shelter. The heavy steel doors were closed and we all found our seats on the wooden benches along the walls.

Each family group had its name plates above its seats. We had five spaces. We were safe there. I stored my violin case under my seat. The temperature in the shelter was an even sixty-five degrees year-round. I talked with some neighbor children for a while and then dozed off, leaning my head against

Mother's shoulder.

After the air raid was over some of the men, designated for this job, inspected the neighborhood and gave their report before anyone was released from the shelter.

The men told us that many homes had been swept away by air mines. They strike sideways and take everything above ground with them. They seldom make a crater. Other homes were hit with fire bombs and were in flames. Some of the home owners were allowed to go to their burning houses to put out the fires with sand. We had buckets of "fire sand" on every floor of our house. It was impossible for the fire departments to extinguish thousands of fires after an air raid.

A staff bomb from a British plane had fallen through the stone overhang of our front door. It burned out on the stone walkway without causing any harm.

One of the scouts, the men who had evaluated the damage in the neighborhood, made this announcement. "All people living in Sonnenberg Street number 46 to 59 may not go home. We found a bomb crater there. It is in front of house number fifty-five. The bomb has not exploded. It may be a time bomb."

Number fifty-five was our house.

Those neighbors who had no place to go, stayed in the shelter. Our family took off for the hospital where Father worked. On our way down the street we had to climb over fallen electrical wires. We stumbled over all kinds of debris. Our eyes burned from the smoke. We passed burning houses, people trying to save some of their belongings, dead and wounded lying on the sidewalk. We felt the heat of the burning city. The night sky was blood red. The fire storm came racing toward us. Hot ash fell from the sky and covered our bodies.

We arrived at the hospital. It was also badly damaged. But what was this? All personnel including nurses, doctors, maids and foreign prisoners of war had formed a human chain handing water buckets to each other trying to extinguish the flames in the Nurses Home. Their efforts were in vain. The beautiful building burned to the ground.

We slept a few hours in the bunk beds of the hospital shelter.

The next morning Mother and I struggled through all the debris to reach our house. It was still standing, this strong, stone building. The bomb had not exploded. But as we came closer we saw a German soldier guarding the area. He carried a gun over his shoulder and protected the neighborhood. Mother and I quietly climbed over back fences and finally reached the house. What a shambles. No windows, no doors, furniture smashed. We did not stop to look at all the damage, after all, the bomb could have exploded at any moment. The only reason we went home was to see if our canary, Hansel, had survived. His cage hung in our "winter garten," a glassed-in veranda in the back of the house. Hansel was still alive. I climbed on a chair and unhooked the cage from the still swinging chain fastened to the ceiling. Poor birdie. I covered the cage with the "cozy" which bore the embroidered words "Gute Nacht, Hansel" (Good night, Hansel). We always covered his cage at night. Mother reached for the box of seeds and we quickly climbed back over the various fences and ran to the hospital.

My sisters and I stayed in one of the patient's rooms, while my parents slept in Father's office on two couches. During the four weeks we stayed there, we had ample time to help with the cleanup of the hospital and park. We had no electricity or water. The operating-room and other essential rooms in the hospital were lit by a generator.

For water we formed another "human chain," this time to the nearby spring. All day we helped pass the buckets. This crisis was especially difficult for the kitchen and laundry. Somehow they had to keep going.

My sister Siglinde helped in the lab. She learned to take blood from the patients and did some of the microscopic work. When she found something interesting, like a streptococcus, she called Christa and me. We eagerly looked through the microscope into the world of tiny viruses that attack people from within.

I also helped carry food trays to the patients and Christa played with the sick children. During these war years some older but healthy folks lived at the hospital. One lady was the widow of an industrialist. She had been a patient many times and was well known by doctors and nurses. She had lost all her belongings and now lived in a hospital room.

I also remember an old gentleman. He was in his nineties and held the title of privy counsellor. This was a highly respected position under the last king of Wuerttemberg. He had a private nurse, Schwester Marga. All nurses are called Schwester, which means sister in English. The profession of nurse is known as Krankenschwester (sister to the sick).

One day I was privileged to bring him his dinner. He asked me who I was and was pleased when I told him that I was the director's daughter.

Among the prisoners of war who worked in the hospital kitchen and park were two Russians and a Norwegian sailor. The latter was captured in 1940 when the Germans invaded Norway. He wore his blue sailor uniform all during the war and returned to his country in 1945. He was such a handsome young man. He spoke fluent German and I sometimes talked to him.

After four weeks in the hospital we were finally allowed to return to our home. We needed to clean up there. The bomb had been officially declared a dud and posed no further danger if left undisturbed.

It had rained almost every day during those four weeks, and the bomb sank deeper and deeper into the muddy soil. We never saw any part of the bomb.

Then one day a military truck arrived and a group of men jumped off. They wore the striped uniforms of political prisoners and were guarded by some armed soldiers. The men grabbed their shovels and began digging. It took them three days before they finally reached the bomb. During those days the people of the neighborhood brought food and drink to the prisoners and guards. We were so thankful for their efforts to rid us of this danger. They risked their lives to do so. I remember taking the men bottles of apple cider and bread. Sophie, who ran a little milk and cheese shop, came over with some buttermilk and cottage cheese for them. The men appreciated the gift of food. Political prisoners could volunteer for this kind of work. If they survived three excavations of unexploded bombs they were freed.

Now came the most difficult part of the whole undertaking. The bomb had to be pulled out and defused. The men put a heavy rope around the five-ton monster. Then slowly, slowly, the truck moved and pulled the bomb out. I watched from our balcony for a while, but then we were told by means of a bullhorn to take cover in the cellar until further notice.

We listened. Maybe the bomb would explode after all, we whispered as we waited by candlelight. Electricity had again been turned off. We had endured two more air raids in the few days just before the dud was removed. This time another part of the city was destroyed.

We wanted to thank the men for their good deed, but the truck with the bomb had already left. A few days later the city employees repaired the broken water pipe, filled in the crater, blacktopped the street and the whole incident became just one more exciting war memory.

Chocolate and My Ruined Bicycle

From my war diary:

Around noon on April 10, 1945, the accident occurred. It happened one day after my sixteenth birthday. I cannot believe that I risked my life for two little boxes of chocolate. Thank God! The driver of the car was uninjured, but his car and my bike were demolished.

Well, I have fairly well recovered from my leg injury, but my head still hurts and memories are lacking, mainly short term memories. The doctor told me it may be several months before I will be cured from the severe concussion. He also advised me not to read as of yet. It would strain my eyes too much. However, the doctor recommended that I sit by the window and look at the green leaves in the garden. Green is a soothing, cool color. I am glad he gave me this advice.

On April 10, at seven o'clock in the morning, my family listened to the news. A radio announcer had this to say: "The Stollwerk Chocolate Factory in Gaisburg will open today at nine o'clock. Every person under eighteen or over sixty years of age will receive a box of chocolate. Bring your ration card for sugar. The factory will be open until one p.m. only."

What exciting news!

I felt sorry though for my sister Sigline. She had turned eighteen in February. She was too old. "Anyway," she said, "I would never enjoy eating chocolate that was meant for our fighting men." She huffed these words as she stormed out of the room. Siglinde's outburst did not impress me. She was just too patriotic.

"I wish I could go," I sighed. "Chocolate would be the perfect late birthday gift for me, but going to Gaisburg for it?" I was not too sure.

Gaisburg was a suburb about six miles away. I would have to walk up our hilly street, cross the forest, and walk down that steep, steep path to Gaisburg. (That path was so steep, only adults were allowed to go sledding there in winter . . . and no vehicles were allowed either.) It would take me over two hours to get there. Then I would have to find the factory, stand in line, and return home. It would be an all day undertaking.

"You may best forget about this plan. No way will I permit you to venture into a part of the city you are totally unfamiliar with, and anyway, it is too dangerous to go. Listen, don't you hear the sirens already howling and it is only seven o'clock in the morning . . ."

Oh, yes, the sirens, our whole lives rotated around the warnings of the sirens. I hated them! Every time I looked forward to a fun outing there were the sirens again, spoiling everything. I listened and counted . . . Aha, three howls. This short, one-minute warning was against dive-bombers only. We knew they could strike anywhere, anytime. If we wanted to run to the shelter every time we heard that short-warning howl, we would not have accomplished anything. So we just took chances. We went about our business like shopping for food and only sought shelter if we were directly attacked. When the enemy planes, the Spitfires dove down at us, their engines screaming and their machine-guns clattering, we raced to the cellar if we were close to home. After all, we did not only have to hide from enemy fire but also from German antiaircraft shells.

Mother was still trying to talk sense into me. "My dear child, I understand your yearning for chocolate. I myself would not turn down a piece. But the enemy planes are here already. Are you not afraid they would shoot at you? Even if you would safely arrive at the Stollwerk Chocolate factory, the long line of people waiting there would be an easy target for the enemy planes."

But these were only individual little air craft. It was more serious when we had a three-minute warning. That was for the Flying Fortress Bombers. We did not waste any time then, but headed for the shelters. These planes, hundreds of them, flew so high that rarely was one shot down by antiaircraft artillery. I remember watching German fighter planes trying to attack the B-17 American Bombers. I heard the bone-chilling noise and witnessed the little white puffy clouds way up in the sky. These puffs were caused by the exploding German and American weapons.

"Besides the planes," Mother continued, "The enemy tanks are only about thirty miles from here. We have listened to their earth shaking thunder for months now. The Allied Combat Forces are so near, they may battle here in our city in a matter of hours or days. And YOU want to risk your life for two little boxes of chocolate? You know all this, so why do I have to repeatedly remind you of the constant dangers we have to live with."

"Oh Mother, you worry too much." I could not admit that Mother knew best.

The doorbell rang. I answered. It was Manfred from next door. He had also heard the morning news. Manfred was fourteen, tall and lanky with blond hair and adventure on his mind.

"Let's get our bikes and go. Maybe we reach the factory by the time it opens at nine. But we must hurry. Frau Schrack said she wants to go, too. She will be ready in a few minutes. We can all go together."

Great. Manfred was such a good neighbor. Frau Schrack was a very attractive "thirty-something" with two wonderful children. Christel, a pretty blonde ten-year-old spoke in a Swiss German dialect. She sounded really cute. Gunther was thirteen. He had been hit by a bomb splinter that tore a big part of muscle from his right leg. He could not join in our ball games anymore. Poor Gunther had to limp along on crutches, but he was always cheerful. We often loaned him our wagon when he had to see his doctor. Frau Schrack was divorced from her Swiss husband and she and the children had moved from Bern, Switzerland, just before the war began.

Mother had given me her long sermon. There was no sense in trying to get her approval. So why not leave right now with my two good neighbors? I thought. I pulled up my kneesocks, put on my shoes and grabbed my jacket.

"Mother, I am going with Manfred and Frau Schrack, we'll take our bikes. Manfred knows the way. Good-bye." I shouted as I flew out the back door, I quickly lowered the family bicycle from its stand. This bike was the only vehicle left. Father's car, an Adler, had to be turned in long ago for war efforts. Public transportation had ceased to exist.

I met the two friends in front of our house. It was a cool morning. We pushed our bikes up the hill. When we arrived at the hairpin curve to the left, I was aware of how narrow the road had become at that point. I had never noticed it before. It had only one usable lane for a short distance, maybe one hundred feet. Why? Because the neighbors had dug their own air-raid shelter into the hillside. They had piled the earth and stones onto the sidewalk and two lanes of the street. No trucks were available to haul away all that debris.

During a previous rain some of that rust-colored dirt had been washed across the only lane still usable. We lifted our bikes to the sidewalk and kept pushing. Finally we reached the top of the steep Richard Wagner Street. In the distance, machine-guns!

We paused for a moment to catch our breath. Manfred pointed in the direction of the firing dive-bombers. We could see them in the distance.

"My goodness, they are attacking that passenger train in the valley!" Frau Schrack was shocked.

I just shrugged, although I felt sorry for the people on the train.

There were only open fields around, no tunnel in sight to hide in. I had experienced attacks like that when all passengers crawled under their seats in panic and paralyzing fear for their lives. I knew that feeling of terror and absolute helplessness.

"Oh well, this train is a few miles away. We might as well go on." I had resigned myself to this insecure life.

But instead of following the open road winding down towards Gaisburg, we chose the steep, steep path at the edge of the woods. "Durchfahren verboten" was the sign that stared at us. "Vehicles prohibited."

We pushed our hand brakes and slowly walked next to our bikes, bracing ourselves. We felt safe from these attacking planes, roaring above us as long as we could stay hidden in the shadows of the forest. The enemy did not see us.

"We are almost there." Manfred assured us. He knew the way. We followed him. He was a good guide.

When we saw the smoke stacks of the Stollwerk Schokolade Company, we knew we had reached our goal at last. As we pedaled around the last corner we saw a crowd waiting at the closed gate. A high wall surrounded the factory. It looked forbidding.

"My goodness, I did not expect this many people." Frau Schrack hesitated.

The crowd seemed restless.

"Oh well, we are used to standing in line," I said matter-of-factly. "Let's park our bikes next to the gate until the manager opens up. It is almost nine o'clock. It won't be too much longer and we will be able to park our vehicles in the guarded courtyard. I will stay with the bikes while you, Manfred, and Frau Schrack stand in line."

This was a good plan.

Nobody would try to steal our bicycles, not with me as their guard. I had control of the situation. My friends had to walk way down to the end of the line.

"I hope we don't have to wait too long before we can get in." I whispered to myself. "What time is it, anyway?" My watch read nine o'clock.

Nothing happened. The gate remained closed. People started to push and shout.

"We have already waited for two hours. Open up. Now!" Some men angrily pounded on the wooden door.

Silence was the answer. The manager made no attempt to open up.

"The newsman was probably wrong. I believe they have no chocolate at all to give away, we might as well go home," a woman in a black coat yelled. Another woman climbed on a big rock in order to be seen and heard by everybody. "These fools in the factory think they can cheat us. We won't stand for it. Let's storm the place and see what they think of that. Power to the people."

The dive-bombers screamed overhead. Machine-guns clattered nearby. The clock ticked on. Finally, I saw a head appearing at the top of the wall. It was the manager's.

He shouted through a bullhorn. "If you don't move back, I cannot open the gate. Stop pushing." He wildly waved his arms. His round face turned blood red and the blue veins on his neck bulged like thick ropes. No one listened to him. Instead of standing in an orderly line the crowd surged forward frantically, angrily shaking fists and screaming insults towards the manager.

I still stood and guarded the bikes. I could not believe the behavior of these people. They were totally out of control.

I found myself engulfed by this sea of maddened humanity. "Oh Lord, please let me get out of here alive," I prayed. "I don't want to get trampled to death by this mob. Mother was right. I should have stayed at home. Forgive me God for disobeying her."

The manager's head disappeared. I tried to wriggle out, but

it was impossible. The mob was angrier than before and yelled and rushed toward the gate.

A moment later a wide ice cold jet of water from a fire hose above the wall shot down and flooded the crowd. Screaming, the people fled in all directions.

I was still guarding the bikes. Standing close to the wall, the jet of water streamed over my head. Still, the spray soaked me from head to toe. My wet hair stuck in strands to my face and I felt ice cold drops trickling down my neck and back. I was deeply humiliated, very deeply.

My friends were out of sight. Had they run away, too? Had they been injured? I had no choice but to wait by our dripping bikes.

Then, suddenly, the gate opened. A small group of survivors of this watery attack slushed its way through the open door and the courtyard to the factory entrance. These people had regained their sanity and behaved like normal human beings once more.

"Mass hysteria can be deadly." This voice behind me sounded familiar.

I turned around and fervently hugged Frau Schrack. Manfred stood dripping behind her.

"You have no idea how thankful I am to see you still alive." I exclaimed.

We parked our vehicles inside the entrance. Cold, wet, and shivering we had to wait again, this time in an orderly fashion.

Finally, we received our hard earned "treasure"—two boxes of Stollwerk Chocolates.

The sirens sounded their "all clear" signal. Thank God, at least we could go home now without worrying about enemy attacks.

I wrung out my little cloth bag, which I had kept in my pocket. It was still damp but I was glad to put everyone's boxes in it. The little bag happily dangled from my handle bar as we three friends triumphantly cycled towards home. We were really pleased with ourselves. We had accomplished our goal. We had prevailed in the face of deadly forces. Water hose, mob, and enemy fire . We had trophies to prove our bravery: two chocolate bars for each of us.

We pushed our bikes up the steep, steep hill and now enjoyed the easy ride down Richard Wagner Street. I was first in line. What a morning this had been, what an adventure. What an exciting story we would tell our families.

"Just slow down at the hairpin curve," I told myself. "Remember the one lane stretch."

I put on the brakes and looked back to see if my friends were also slowing down. They were right behind me. At that moment a sand-colored car came toward me. I froze. I heard no crash, I felt no crash. We collided. I was thrown on top of the dirt hill. In and out of consciousness for moments at a time, I glanced around me. The car lay upside down next to my twisted bicycle. A German officer crawled out from underneath his vehicle. He seemed to be uninjured He must have unsuccessfully tried to avoid the collision by driving his car up the mount of dirt. It must have turned over and rolled down. Opening my eyes for a few seconds, I saw that the car's roof had caved in and the hood had been knocked out of shape.

The next time I became aware, I noticed a liquid running out from underneath the car. It might have been water or gasoline. The officer turned his vehicle right side up onto the street and then he checked me for broken bones. I was still in shock and felt no pain. One of my shoes was missing.

I do not remember walking home the hundred yards. Frau Schrack supported me and Manfred carried the wreckage and broken parts of my bike.

The front wheel resembled a number eight. The handle bar was ripped off, as well as one pedal. The bag with chocolate was later found along with my shoe. A sweet little neighbor girl delivered these to our house. Bless her.

I have no memories of coming home and seeing my family. I only regained consciousness while lying on the blue velvet couch in the children's room. Mother had spread a sheet under my bloody leg and gently wiped my wounds with a cotton ball dipped in camomile tea.

I saw Frau Schrack sitting on a chair next to me and

wondered why she was in my room.

The piercing pain in my leg was the reason I had suddenly woken up. I wished I could have remained in blissful unconsciousness. But the pain threw me back into reality with a vengeance. I had no concept of time.

"What happened?" I mumbled at last.

"Remember? You rode your bike to the chocolate factory and you had an accident on your way home." Mother tried to help me with my lost memory.

But what she said made no sense to me. The trip that morning seemed to have occurred years ago. Mother bandaged my leg loosely and put me to bed. Half asleep, I heard the sirens again—more dive bombers. I could not get up.

Father took me to the hospital the next morning. Mother had padded our trusted wagon with a blanket and she put a pillow behind my head. It was an uncomfortable ride, but it was the best Father could do. Ambulance service had been suspended some time ago.

After being checked for possible broken bones and internal injuries, I was transported to the hospital's shelter, the tunnel in the hillside. Two nurses carefully lifted me onto a bottom bunk. The straw mattress was damp and bumpy. My headache was worse when I opened my eyes, so I kept them closed most of the time. The concussion was severe. The bruise on my leg turned black and it covered me from thigh to ankle. It was excruciating in spite of pain medicine.

The only human contact I had was during air-raids when all patients were brought to the shelter. I was not allowed any visitors. To my delight a little brown mouse appeared occasionally. It glanced at me and then darted away. "What are you poor little creature living on in this dark, empty shelter?" I whispered to myself. "I wish I could feed you some crumbs, but I have none."

One day I again watched the little mouse. This time it climbed up to the top bunk bed across from the aisle and disappeared under the pillow. I heard some rustling of parchment paper, and then my little friend rushed away with something in its mouth. I wondered what it found under that pillow. During the next air-raid, when all patients again had come to the shelter the puzzle was solved. The appetizing aroma of smoked sausage had tickled my nose for some time. I could not figure out what it was. No kitchen had been built into the shelter, but I was familiar with the scent. Of course, it was salami.

Like chocolate this sausage which did not need refrigeration had been issued to the civilian population just days before enemy troops would have plundered all the stores.

Now I knew what the patients were nibbling on every time they felt a twinge of hunger.

I had heard the rustling of parchment paper under bed sheets, noticed the flashing of a pocket knife here and there, watched bits of food disappearing in wide open mouths, and now I knew. The patients were hiding their rations of salami under their bed pillows. They were prepared for The Battle of Stuttgart. Within the next few days—or maybe tomorrow—it would happen. Who knew? Would the cooks be able to prepare any meals? Would we have electricity, gas, and water? How long and how terrifying would this anticipated battle last? Nobody knew the answers.

Crates of bottled water had been stored in the shelter for weeks. It was cool deep down in this underground tunnel. No matter what happened, no one would starve, not as long as we could live on water and salami.

While I lay there in pain I thought about the trip to the chocolate factory. My memory slowly improved and the accident became more real. Yes, I had been foolish to disobey Mother. Yes, I would have avoided the mishap if I had stayed home. I thought about it all the time. I also realized that a Guardian Angel had lifted me onto that dirt hill for a soft fall. Had I been thrown to the other side of the street, I would have been smashed against a high wall and killed.

"Thank you, God, for watching over me and for sending your Guardian Angel. I needed him. I did wrong and I am sorry," I prayed.

All Hell broke loose on April 20 and 21 during the Battle of

Stuttgart. Even the weather was hellish with snowstorms, hail, thunder, and lightning.

We were safe in the shelter and thankful we had some food, water, salami, and bits of chocolate.

April 20, 1933 to 1945

I was born on April 9, but Mother told me that I was due to arrive on April 20. I was eleven days early. Throughout my childhood I believed that I was cheated of a very special birthday celebration. April 20, 1889 was Adolf Hitler's date of birth. He was born and grew up in Braunau, a small Austrian town on the Inn river.

We learned all about him and his struggle to become a German politician after having fought in the German Army during World War I. His beloved Austria, along with many other provinces, had been severed from Germany by the Versailles Treaty in 1918. He dreamed of a Greater Germany, the heart of Europe. His goal was to win back the lost territories and to once more unite the country for all German people.

April 20th became a national holiday after Hitler was elected chancellor in 1933. All public buildings, factories, and businesses were closed. Instead of going to school, we watched the wonderful parades. Political speeches by mayors of every town and city were well attended by enthused citizens.

Stuttgart, the capital of the state of Wuerttemberg was highly decorated with banners and flags on all public buildings as well as homes. Our magnificent troops paraded in their splendid uniforms, stirring our patriotic pride. The Africa Corps in sand-colored uniforms proudly rode their camouflaged tanks decorated with fresh oak branches, the symbol of victory. Marines wore dark blue, infantry gray-green. Rows and rows of them marched to the sound of stirring martial music. The soles of their boots were covered with hobnails, each goose-step echoing the sound of hundreds and hundreds of boots on the cobblestone streets. Children waved their little flags and showered their beloved men in uniform with flowers and sweets.

As a child I did not understand my parents' less than enthusiastic attitudes on such occasions. Our maid, Ellie, always took us to the parades. Father and Mother stayed home. They remembered World War I just twenty-five years earlier. My parents were eighteen years old when that war ended in defeat and disgrace and the country was divided by the victors.

Mother's parents, who had established a successful flower and landscape business in Metz, Lorraine, had to sell everything in a hurry and return to Germany because Metz became French in 1918. Millions of the best men of their generation were dead or crippled by the horrors of war. "We raise our sons in one war to become cannon fodder for the next," was Mother's lamentation.

April 20, 1945. The end of the war was near, that much was certain. There were no parades, no banners or flags fluttered in the morning breeze, no enthusiasm for our leaders was left. Our proud and beloved city, Stuttgart, was a sea of rubble. Thousands of civilian graves were marked by crosses in the ruins of their homes. Old men, mothers, and children had burned to death in the deadly flames of phosphorous bombs, phosphor from which no one could escape. It burned on every surface: wood, stone, asphalt, iron bridges, and rivers. Our Holocaust was fire and explosive bombs that tore apart buildings as well as human beings and animals. The whole country was transformed into one giant, endless and gruesome graveyard.

Yes, this was April 20, 1945. Our Fuehrer, Adolf Hitler, was dead. "He died for his country's glory while leading his brave troops against the barbarous Russian Communists." That is what we read in the newspaper. Much later the occupying Allied troops told us that he had poisoned himself in his bunker in Berlin. His companion, Eva Braun, died with him. Their ashes were scattered over the land.

No statue, no memorial can be found anywhere. We burned his book *Mein Kampf* along with his photographs. We buried our Hitler Youth uniforms and flags. We destroyed political documents, anything that reminded us of the reign of this man.

But I could not burn my War Diary. I simply could not. I hid it under my mattress and did not open it for thirty years. It was too painful to be reminded us of the war and its aftermath.

Again, this was April 20, 1945. My family was at home listening to Dr. Goebbels. He was the propaganda minister and gave his radio speech every Friday night. He encouraged the German people not to give up hope for an eventual victory. We were surrounded from all sides by enemies. How could a victory be possible? He ended his address with these words. "We shall win this great battle. We will allow the enemy to cross the Rhine river, but then we shall use our new weapon. This weapon is so powerful, we shall destroy all our enemies in one day."

Was he talking about the Atom Bomb? Everything was kept such a secret. We knew that our scientists were feverishly working to perfect an atomic bomb. Dr. Goebbels was later hanged with our other leaders after the Nuremberg Trials.

It was now eleven o'clock at night. My parents had just turned off the radio and shuddered as they heard the screaming and explosions as the first enemy artillery shells fell in the woods behind our home. Then the sirens sounded louder and longer than usual. This was the end. My parents knew there was no hope for a victory. They quickly loaded our wagon with pillows and blankets. Christa ran to the living room to get the cage and Hansel's food. They all ran to the hospital shelter. I had been in that shelter since April 10th, when I had my bicycle accident, and Siglinde had started to work in the hospital laboratory. Thank God, the whole family was together in the shelter, safe.

Right after all patients and personnel were in the tunnel, the heavy steel doors were locked.

In a desperate attempt to save the city from enemy tanks, all bridges were blown up. Everything came crashing down, from the high Autobahn bridges to the smallest pedestrian crossings. The bombs, the machine guns, the antiaircraft artillery, enemy shells, explosions. It was hell! It did not stop at all that night.

Father was told over the police phone that enemy tanks were already in the suburbs and some had been spotted on the main road to the city.

Father announced. "We were just informed by the police that the French and Senegalese troops and their tanks will be here by daybreak. We do not know how long the German military can defend us. We will all remain in the shelter until the war for us is over. Please hide your valuables under your mattresses and stay calm. We were told that the Senegalese soldiers are allowed to steal anything they want. We will try everything to keep them out of the shelter."

A baby boy was born that night in the tunnel's delivery room.

Just then, two very young and frightened German soldiers came running to the shelter. They were pale as ghosts and begged for civilian clothes and a place to hide. They were afraid to become prisoners of war. Both requests were fulfilled. They hid way back in the tunnel where rows of benches were lined up. This area had the nickname, "Train Express." It was sixty feet under ground and very safe. What I did not like about this "train" was the air-shaft that reached all the way to the top of the hill and ended in a private garden. This shaft was needed for fresh air. Although the "train" was the safest place to be during air-raids, the outside noises came straight down the air-shaft to were we all huddled.

The noises of bombs, artillery, explosions, sirens and machine guns were too much for me. I stayed with Father in his Control Room.

As the afternoon of the second day of the Battle of Stuttgart progressed, Father and a doctor walked through the tunnel to the hospital. What a sight.. All floors and beds were covered with glass and wood splinters from doors and furniture. The electricity had been turned off.

As the two men looked out the window, they saw a couple of German soldiers with their machine guns.

"We will defend the hospital," they yelled up to my father.

"Oh no, you won't," Father called back. "Go and defend the ruins across the street but get away from here as quickly as you can. The soldiers disappeared.

The international sign for a military hospital is the Red Cross. Large signs were painted on roofs and sides of these buildings. Our hospital was civilian. Therefore it bore the sign of a large red square on a white background on the roof and walls. The enemy planes were supposed to honor these signs and not destroy these buildings. Thank God the German soldiers with their machine guns fled. Had they stayed to defend the hospital and shot at the enemy, it would have been the end of us all.

Father saw the first Allied tank rolling down the street in front of the hospital. A French officer and some Senegalese soldiers jumped off and came running to the hospital. Father quickly tore a sheet from a patient's bed and waved it out a window as a sign of surrender. But the officer ignored this sign and shouted, "Where are the soldiers, where are the weapons? I will shoot you if you do not tell me the truth. I shall count to ten. Tell me the truth or you will die. 1-2-3-4-5-6-7-8-9-10."

Father answered as calmly as he could. "There are no soldiers or weapons. This is a civilian hospital."

"Then, where are the patients, I do not see any." The French officer became impatient.

"They are all in the bunker. Many have infectious diseases." Father tried desperately to keep the black soldiers away from the patients. The officer waved his troops to check the shelter. When they saw the rows of bunk beds with the sick, the whole tunnel just barely lit by a few lightbulbs, they turned around and left. We were so relieved.

The Battle of Stuttgart lasted two days, then the mayor surrendered to the Allied troops. There was no sense in fighting on. This was the end of the war for us.

The Unconditional Surrender of Germany did not come until May 8, 1945, Father's forty-fifth birthday. We now had no government, no military, no police to protect us. We were totally at the mercy of the occupying forces. And we were afraid for the future.

"Better an end with horror, than horror without end." These were Father's sad words.

My War Diary
(Note: All photos throughout
this book are from my war diary.)

Syterlin Script: I learned in first grade and used until the end of World War II. After that, this script was outlawed by the foreign military who occupied Germany and who were unable to read handwritten papers. We had to learn a new, internationally used script. My whole war diary was written in Syterlin. Here is a sample of the alphabet.

Heilbronn, den 7.7.1944

Die Engländer und Nordamerikaner haben, wenn auch nur langsam, in Frankreich vordringen können. Sie haben schon Cherbourg im Port Hand. (Nord d. 12). Es gilt zu mir noch ein großer Vorentscheidungs... stärker Besetzungen der Atlantikwall gelingt es dem Feind weiter noch träge vorzudringen.

Im Osten stehen wir wieder, wie vor 2 Jahren vor der ... Die Frühjahrsschlacht hat weit weg in bälde wieder in ...

... und ist in Italien. Nachdem wir uns vor den deutschen Truppen zu ... ist (g ... bis Mai-Juni) kommen Amerikaner und ... weiter nach Norden vor.

37.

Heilbronn, d. 8.6.44.

Nun hat die Invasion tatsächlich begonnen. Wir haben nun schon seit Herbst 1943 darauf gewartet. Nun sind sie gerade am Atlantikwall, der starken Befestigung an der Küste Frankreichs, gelandet. Hoffentlich fassen die Löcher neuen Luftlandetruppen nicht festen Fuß. Es ist zu nun ein furchtbarer Kampf dort oben in der nordwestküste von Frankreich. Uns alles gut ... und die Feinde nicht durch Frankreich hindurch kommen und Deutschland.

36.

My War Diary

When I was thirteen years old, my Aunt Marta sent me an empty book with the idea that I may use it for a diary. She said in her birthday card, "My dear godchild, you are now at an age when you may write about very private experiences in this book. In years to come you will look back on your teenage secrets and read about long forgotten memories. May you experience much joy and happiness doing so."

But I grew up in an increasingly dangerous war, and so I decided to write—instead of private secrets—about World War II and how it affected our very existence. Of course it is written in German. Here is the translation.

March 9th, 1943
    Every day a famous quote is given in the newspaper. Today's is by Friedrich Schiller: "War is a rough and violent craft, one cannot get by using gentle means." British air-raid

*against Nuremberg. Since these attacks are against helpless
civilians, they are called "terror attacks."*

~

March 10th, 1943
*"All strength of man is acquired in battle with himself
and by conquest of self." (Fichte)*
Terror attack against Munich.

~

March 11th, 1943
*"An appeal to fear will never find an echo in the German
heart." (Bismarck) U-boats sink 36 ships with 207,000 tons
in twenty-four hours.*

~

March 12th, 1943
*Last night the British Air Force executed a terror attack
on Stuttgart. At 10:30 p.m. the sirens howled. We jumped up
from sleep, dressed quickly and ran to the cellar which is our
air-raid shelter. We had hardly arrived there when the
antiaircraft artillery started to shoot. We heard the roaring of
the bombs, then the explosions which were followed by the typical
strong concussions. Suddenly machine-guns clattered, perhaps
those were board-weapons of enemy planes.*

*This attack did not happen in our part of town, and so
we peeped out the front door. Of course, no lights were on in
houses or streets. What a drama presented itself to us. The
whole inner city was lit brightly by hundreds of flares hanging
and slowly descending from little parachutes. Here and there
we saw searchlights racing across the night sky and listened to
the roar of bombers and German fighter planes.*

*We girls stood paralysed with terror. We had never
witnessed horror like this. Our parents finally called us back
into the safety of the cellar. Electricity had been shut off and so
we sat in the darkness until we found a candle to sparingly
light our surrounding area where we huddled. We were below*

ground. The air-shafts at ground level were covered with sacks filled with sand. In peace time the shafts could be opened to get fresh air into the cellar and closed during rain or winter weather.

We sat, motionless in our shelter and listened to the eerie sound of the sand trickling from the bags on the air-shafts. Then suddenly a thrust of wind, called concussion, slammed against the front door and heavy cellar door. We knew then that a heavy bomb had fallen for the first time in our neighborhood.

Finally the shooting became less and less and then stopped. We stepped outside. What a sight. Between the little park where we used to play and Lohr's house the sky was blood red—in the middle of the night. The suburbs of Heslach, Vaihingen and Moehringen were hard hit. At one a.m. the sirens' long one minute sound told us that all was well.

We now could go back to bed. It was hard falling asleep. The next day, school did not resume. There was too much damage all around. Near the Bubenbad a torpedo hit, but did not explode, thank God. But even so there was much damage done to homes and businesses. This included our best bakery and Cafe Bubenbad. What a shame, it was such an elegant place.

Stalingrad, the worst battle of the war was fought here.

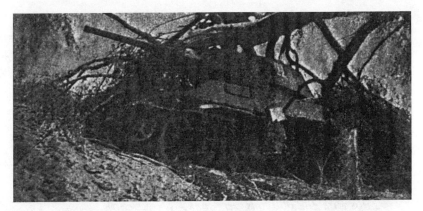

Destroyed Russian tank.

Dates of "Terror Attacks" 1943-1944. After 1944 I did not count them any longer.

*In our neighborhood we found many of the little parachutes
on which the flares hung to light the area for the enemy planes
to drop their bombs. Many bombs had fallen into the woods
surrounding Stuttgart. Two time bombs exploded on Friday,
one at 9 a.m. and one at 11:30 a.m. The last one in
Bopserwald Str.*

~

March 13,1943
*"Bitter street battles in some part of Charkov, Russia.
Thirty enemy planes were shot down. In three days forty-seven
ships with 282,000 tons were sunk." (News clip)*

~

March 15,1943
Charkov is again in German hands.

~

March 16,1943
*"In real life as in fairy-tales, one may not turn around
and look back if one wants to safely get through the dangers of
the pathway. Look straight ahead and rogues will yield. Look
back and you turn into a rock." (Raabe).*
Today, fifty-six Soviet planes were shot down.

Terror attacks on Stuttgart:
March 2, 1943
March 11-12
April 14-15
September 6
October 7-8
November 26
February 20-21, 1944
March 1-2
March 15-16
July 24-25
July 25-26
July 27-28

July 28-29

The last four were the worst, because we had no rest. Lacking also were water, electricity, and gas. The whole city burned, and yet the bombs kept falling. Hell could not be any worse. I wanted to die, I was too exhausted to move, but Father carried me to the hospital shelter. We have to live at the hospital now, because a bomb has fallen in front of our house but did not explode. The whole neighborhood was evacuated because we do not know whether it is a dud or a time bomb.

September 5th was another air-raid. After that I did not keep track of the days very closely. Almost every day the alarm sounded and the bombs fell. It became a way of life. All together we had to endure 179 major terror-attacks on our beautiful city. Every day trains were attacked as well by dive-bombers. I was shot at while riding my bike in the country, but I was able to jump off my bicycle and find shelter in a ditch, shaded by huge fruit trees that grew along the road.

This attack on me occurred between Weil-im-Dorf and Gerlingen. We had purchased a piece of property there, and I was on my way to water the tomato plants.

March 2, 1944

"In the early morning hours of March 12th, British bombers again attacked Stuttgart with mines, explosive bombs, fire bombs, and phosphorus bombs. Heavy damage was done to residential areas as well as cultural and historic buildings. The civilian population suffered many losses." (News clip)

During this air-raid our neighborhood was hard hit for the first time. Up the hill from us at the corner of Sonnenberg Str. a bomb hit the house next to Strohmeier's. It is totally destroyed. A huge bomb fell in Frau Leiner's garden and many more bombs landed in the forest behind that area. Also many fire bombs fell.

Many of our windows are blown out. The doors have only frames left. Many of our walls are cracked and our roll-shutters are torn. A fire bomb hit the overhang of the entrance door, fell through to the cement walk and burned out without damage. A black spot is still visible.

It is cold without windows. We hung blankets over the openings to keep the cold out and the flying ashes. The fires are still burning and the stench is terrible. Also, the smoke hurts our eyes and noses, and the ashes keep falling on our area when the wind shifts. We have a lot of cleaning up to do. Many of the glass splinters are deeply embedded in the furniture and walls. Our Japanese vase was lifted from the radio where it usually stands. It was put down on the buffet without getting broken. That is what concussion can do.

Our silk lamp shade above the dining room table is shredded completely. A bomb splinter was embedded in the pantry door frame. I tried to remove it and keep it as a souvenir, but could not. It will be stuck there forever.

During that air-raid, while we were still in the cellar, we heard a loud noise upstairs, and when we later went back upstairs we found that the big sewing machine and its heavy cabinet had fallen over and were broken.

Concussion does strange things. It is a strong gust of wind that follows every falling bomb and does as much or more damage than the bombs themselves.

We found many splinters from bombs and flak, but the bomb splinters are more valuable than the flak because they are from the enemy. We trade two small ones for one big one.

The water was again turned off for several days because of damage to the pipes. We had to go to the drinking fountain which is spring-fed and runs continually. Before the air-raid Mother had soaked a big load of wash, but she was unable to get it done because the electricity also was turned off. So we all helped to get the wash done by hand. I walked with two big buckets in our wagon all day, standing in line and getting enough water for the big sheets and clothing to get washed. Siglinde and Christa helped too. Doing all this hard work without the help of the washing machine was something we were not used to getting done. Especially wringing out the water from the bed sheets was exhausting, but we got it done.

Later, the Red Cross truck came by and brought us drinking

water and hot soup. The soup was cooked in a big kettle like the soldiers use. Everyone received a potful and it tasted really good. It felt strange to stand in line for free food and Mother sent me to get our share. She could not bring herself to do this.

We did not have gas for a long time. When electricity was turned back on we took two bricks, wedged the flat iron upside down between them, plucked the iron in and this became our cooking surface. It worked really well.

We also found that when we turned our electric space heaters, wires up, we also could use them for cooking. But the milk boiled over once, and that was the end of the little blue heater which Father used in his study.

Gas is always restored last. I do not know why. Perhaps the reason is that gas is made out of coal and it takes longer to produce. Our cooking stove is heated by gas on the left side, and it is a wood or coal burning stove on the right. We use the right side often in winter because it also heats the kitchen.

Our hot water heater also uses gas. It is a big copper thing hanging on the kitchen wall. Water pipes run through it. One provides water for the faucet in the bath tub, the other goes in the opposite direction and heats the water for use in the kitchen. A pilot light always burns, and when we need hot water in either the kitchen or the bath, we turn the gas handle to 'on.' The gas flames heat the water pipes. The slower we let the water run the hotter it is.

We always watch the moon. During new moon when it is very dark, we seldom worry about enemy planes. But on nights when the moon is full we count on having to get up. I sleep in my clothes most nights and wear my treasured wristwatch day and night. I keep my violin case and my shoes next to my bed. Sometimes I do not have time to put my shoes on because the sirens were late in waking us. Often I get a stomach ache and my whole body shudders, even when I do not feel cold. Mother says it is my nerves, as it is very damaging for young girls to be torn out of a deep sleep by the screaming of sirens all around. I am so tired. I wish I could sleep one night without worrying. Why does the enemy destroy our cities?

Governor Murr welcomes wounded soldiers home.

March 6,1944

"Wounded soldiers are exchanged." (U.S. and German prisoners of war.)

A welcome home party was given by the Hitler Youth groups and Party Women's organizations. The troops were welcomed home after having been imprisoned in the U.S.A.

We performed folk dances and sang uplifting songs and one man played the accordion all evening. The soldiers were wounded, some had bandaged eyes, some had their legs amputated. I think they enjoyed our program. We presented them with flowers, cigarettes, and sweets.

They came home to destroyed cities. They were shocked to find Stuttgart in ruins. Our governor, Mr. Murr, gave a speech. He reminded all of us that there is little difference between soldiers fighting on the "outer front," while civilians endure the "inner front."

The young Red Cross helpers prepared an excellent chicken soup and the soldiers ate it with gusto.

May 17, 1944

All school-age children between six and sixteen years of age had to be evacuated from Stuttgart because of the air-raids. All schools are closed. Those students who had relatives in smaller towns or in the country had the choice of living there or being transported by special trains to live in camps specially erected for them and their teachers.

Oma Wintterle, Mother's mom, agreed to have Christa and me living with her. In the same house, downstairs, live Uncle Paul, Aunt Margarita (who is from Madrid, Spain) and cousin Paul, their son. He is nine years old.

Mother and we two sisters came to Heilbronn by train, each carrying a heavy suitcase.

The town of about 50,000 inhabitants is quite nice. Here is no war damage. Christa and I go to High School. I am in the fourth year of High School and Christa is in the second. We do not know how long we have to stay here. Siglinde, who is seventeen had to quit school and was sent to a small village in the Black Forest to help a mother with four children.

The family was bombed out in Stuttgart, and they were moved to the country into a vacant house. The Party helps these families who have to relocate and sends young high school age girls to live with them and help them take care of the children and house work. The lady's husband is fighting on the Eastern Front in Russia.

Christa and I go home every weekend. It is a two hour train trip between Heilbronn and Stuttgart, but sometimes it takes much longer. Last weekend out train was attacked by enemy planes. Luckily we were near a tunnel and the train stopped there until the enemy planes left.

The enemy was fooled for quite some time. Because the first air-raids always happened at night, someone had the clever idea to build a "mock-up" of the huge train station of Stuttgart about twenty miles out of town in the open fields. The structure was very low to the ground, hardly visible from the air, but at night everything was lit up with red and blue light just like a real railroad station. This area was bombed many times much to the disgust of the farmers, whose crops were damaged.

If only Oma's cellar were better. There is no emergency exit here, which bothers me. We often have alarms at night, but so far no air-raids have occurred.

Christa is well off. She was allowed to return home to our parents for health reasons. During the winter of 1943-44 she suffered terribly from bronchitis. She had high fevers and the doctor told us she should not stay here in Heilbronn because of the foggy and damp weather.

The doctor wrote a permit for Christa to return to Stuttgart. I have to stay here another year. I hope the war is over by then and we are all still alive.

Uncle Paul has a big florist business here in Heilbronn, but he has to grow mainly vegetables now. Flowers are a luxury and allowed only for church decorations and funerals. Some nuns come each Saturday to buy flowers for their altars. Usually they bring some food for payment. I saw them hiding a bottle of oil under their capes the other day. One was for Oma, the other bottle for Uncle Paul and his family.

All of Uncle Paul's helpers now are prisoners of war. There are two Polish men, both are called Joseph. One is bigger than the other so we call him Big Joseph, the other Little Joseph. They do not speak much German.

And then there is Monsieur Hardy. He is a French officer. He was allowed to bring his wife from France. Madame Hardy has bleached blonde hair and wears lipstick. She speaks no German. The Hardy's have a room upstairs. Monsieur works in the garden while madame helps Aunt Margarita with cooking for all these men. She is a good cook and knows how to kill chickens and rabbits. She stretches the rabbits' furs on old picture frames to dry and then she makes mittens out of them. They keep the workers' hands warm in winter.

Uncle Paul and Aunt Margarita speak fluent English, German, Spanish, and French, so the Hardys are treated like friends not enemies. Christa and I learned to say "good night" in French, and each night before retiring we say, "Bon soir, Monsieur Hardy, bon soir, Madame Hardy." It does sound *funny to us, hearing ourselves speaking French.*

We have to be polite to all workers. After all, they are no criminals, just prisoners of war.

~

May 10, 1944

"Terror Attack against Munich. Art treasures are destroyed in spite of heroic attempts to save them. During peace times many Englishmen visited Munich as "the city of great culture and art with four stars. Now everything is gone. Especially hard hit was the beautiful State Library on Ludwig Str. But many other buildings are only smoke-blackened ruins." (News clip)

~

June 6, 1944

"Rome, Italy was delivered into American hands by German troops." (News clip)

For a year we expected an invasion by the Americans. All our boys who are between fifteen and seventeen years of age have left to build the West Wall, a fortification along Northern France. Today, June 6th, the newspaper told us the following:

"For weeks heavy bombardment of Northern France along the Atlantic Coast was followed by an invasion of British and US troops in the early morning hours. Shortly after midnight paratroopers were observed in the areas of Trouville, Caen, Cherbourg, and Le Havre. Heavy bombing occurred in the area of Calais-Dunkirk. Heavy fire and exploding mines caused great losses among the enemy. Waves upon waves of enemy paratroopers are landing."

~

June 7, 1944

In the early afternoon hours enemy landing crafts tried to get a foot hold on land by using the protection of artificial fog. Many of the British troops using rubber boats surrendered waving white towels. They were taken as prisoners of war." (News clip)

Heilbronn, June 9, 1944

The invasion has actually begun. We have waited for it since Fall of 1943. The enemy has landed on the Atlantic Wall, the strongest fortification in Northern France. I hope the paratroopers will not get a hold on the area. If only the war could end soon, and the enemy will not come through France into Germany.

~

July 7, 1944

The British and U.S. troops are slowly but surely advancing in France. Cherbourg is already in their hands. The city is one big heap of rubble. In spite of all the fortifications the enemy is able to continue South.

In the East our troops are—as they were two years ago— near Minsk, Russia. The hotly embattled city will soon be in Russian hands once again. The front in Italy is not any better. After Rome fell to the Americans in May, US and Moroccan troops are advancing North.

Our country is on all sides surrounded by enemy troops.

Heilbronn, September 7, 1944

After all these weeks I want to write some more in my diary. During the summer holidays I went home to Stuttgart and had the pleasure of experiencing four terror attacks on our part of the city.

After the first one we found that a dud had landed in the curb between our house and Herr Schuetz's vineyard. The concussion blew out all our windows and doors. We are not allowed to go into our house to save some things because the dud may have been a time bomb and could explode any time. We stayed in the hospital shelter.

The next morning Mother and I sneaked through back yards and over fences and reached the back door to the kitchen entrance. The door was locked but the window was broken and so I carefully climbed through the window opening and tried to avoid getting cut by glass splinters.

Mother and I rescued our canary, Hansel. Some German soldiers guarded the street and turned away homeowners who tried to get to their houses.

We heard time bombs exploding around us and in the forest for two weeks. The hospital windows are also broken and we all help with the cleanup there.

Luckily it is summer. Again we are without water, gas, and electricity. The next night we slept in an empty patients' room. It has no glass in the window and the stench of burning buildings and the noise of explosions are all around us.

Our city was attacked again that night. The sirens were unusable because of the lack of electricity. We had finally gone to sleep, exhausted, when we were rudely chased again out of our beds. The Antiaircraft artillery warned us that enemy planes again are en route to Stuttgart.

I wanted to die. I was too exhausted to get up, but Father carried me to the hospital shelter as the bombs fell again. The same area was the target. Baeuerle's Apothecary across from the hospital was destroyed this time. The Baeuerle's two daughters were buried in the rubble for two days, then they were rescued. The whole city was one cloud of smoke and fires were everywhere.

Two more air-raids followed in the next two nights. Hell cannot be worse. I will never forget the burning of the St. Leonhard's Church which was built in the 14th century. The tower burned for a long time, then it began to sway and finally it crashed into the inferno below.

All night long people whose homes were destroyed walked by. They had wrapped themselves in wet blankets. Many had no hair, it had been burned off. Thousands died and were left in the ruins. Later on crosses were placed where whole families were killed. Men, women, and children together in one mass grave.

Some pets arrived at our door looking for shelter. Christa and I took in a little cat. Mother was sick in the hospital and Father was on a business trip. We fed it some milk and bread. When the sirens howled again, we put it in a duffle bag and *took it to the shelter. We stored the bag under our seats and worried that it might make noises or try to get out. But it remained quiet. After sitting in the shelter for two hours we could finally go home again. We opened the bag and the kitten ran away, never to be seen again. Poor thing.*

We also kept two orphaned turtles for a while. But since we had no food for them we took them to our property in Gerlingen. There they ate the lettuce and strawberries. They overwintered in the compost pile.

In the meantime a second invasion took place in the South of France. British and American troops landed in the area of Toulouse and Cannes. They advanced quick as lightning. In the North the enemy took Paris, Verdun and arrived in Metz, Mother's birth place.

When westerly winds blow, we can hear the thundering of the battlefields. Last Saturday, Uncle Albert and Aunt Marta arrived in Heilbronn from Lorchingen. They had fled there from Silesia to get away from the Russian front. Now they had to flee from the Western enemies.

It won't be long now and the enemy will be in our country, and we will have to flee too. But where could we go? We are surrounded by enemies. In the East, the Russians are in Prussia. In the South-East they fight near the Hungarian border, in the South near Switzerland and in the West near the Rhine.

On top of everything else there was an attempt by some officers to kill Hitler on July 20, 1944. He was injured, but not seriously. Klaus von Stauffenberg and other officers who were found guilty where shot to death.

~

Stuttgart, November 2, 1944

I have been back in my beloved Stuttgart for about four weeks. I will not go back to Heilbronn where I had lived with Oma for over a year. My beautiful home town looks more like a heap of rubble than the proud city of history and culture.

The last two air-raids occurred in one night, October 19th

- 20th. In front of our shelter five or six heavy explosive bombs fell and two air-mines as well. Air-mines fall sideways and erase everything that is above ground, while explosive bombs cause huge craters. People came running to the shelter, screaming. The bombs had fallen before they could reach the shelter in the hillside. Frau Pfleiderer, wife of our shoemaker and Herr Bessler were killed in front of the shelter by the air concussion which tore their lungs to pieces. Shoemaker Pfleiderer was hit by a bomb splinter and died soon after. Mr. Bessler left a wife and eight children behind. The youngest, Giselher was only a baby and Jochen the oldest at fifteen, had just come down with polio. Poor people, all tragedy hit them at one time. They also lost their home that night.

For the time being we have to "camp" in our children's room. It is the only one usable until the carpenters come and get the other rooms repaired.

The house of director Hahn has totally vanished, there is nothing left. Director Hahn is imprisoned because he somehow was involved in the attempt on Hitler's life.

Jaeckle's and Kenngott's houses are also gone and many more in our neighborhood.

Stuttgart—April 3, 1945

"Stuttgart has to evacuate." With this cry we were awakened on the Tuesday after Easter at five-thirty in the morning. Herr Kirchdoerfer screamed this message all over our neighborhood. He had been notified by the Party because he is in charge of our area.

The Kirchdoerfers are very active in the Party and were responsible for this order being obeyed. They were the first ones to burn all their "Nazi stuff" in the courtyard. Books, pictures of Hitler, uniforms, letters, medals, and other items. We did the same. The Kirchdoerfers left with the last train out of Stuttgart. But where are we supposed to go? News came that the enemy tanks were already in Bietigheim or Ludwigsburg, about 20 miles away. We did not know what rumors to believe.

The whole city swarmed like a disturbed bee hive. People were running here and there, some left the city by bicycle, others pulled carts with belongings, some stayed in the shelters.

We packed our suitcases and grabbed our pillows. Then we hurried to the Bethesda Hospital bunker. There was a rumor about a train leaving from the North Terminal to carry people who wanted to leave to the country. This terminal is about 15 miles from where we lived. The main train station has long been destroyed. People gathered at the North Terminal by the thousands, but no train came. Then the enemy dive-bombers started shooting at these refugees and many died there from their terrible injuries.

At this point we do not care anymore who wins this war. We just want the slaughter to end.

Those citizens who wanted to leave to the country or the mountains have left, and we who had planned to stay here gradually calmed down and continued our struggle to stay alive. Only the constant thunder and vibration from the Western battlefields remind us that the enemy is near.

∼

April 10,1945

My story "Chocolate and My Ruined Bike," tell about what occurred that day.

∼

April 20th and 21st

The enemy shells whistle, then they explode. We can see where they come from. Across the city, behind the Hasenberg, a wooded hill.

The night before the enemy conquered Stuttgart we patients did not sleep an eye full. The German soldiers detonated all bridges, and the enemy bombs and artillery exploded all around us. We were again transported to the bunker. We stayed the night while outside the Battle of Stuttgart raged. (More in my story "April 20th, 1933-45.")

Aftermath of World War II
& Foreign Occupation

Hiding Our Valuables

I remember the day I came home from school in spring of 1943. Mother sat on the floor in front of the heavy oak buffet and packed up her good china. While tears streamed down her face she carefully wrapped each piece in newspaper before tightly packing it in a wooden box.

"Mutti, oh Mutti, what are you doing?" I was upset.

Mother quickly dried her tears.

"We have a chance today to send all our valuables to the country. A minister friend of Father's offered to store everything in the deep cellar of his country church. A truck will soon be here to take all these boxes away. Our mattresses, featherbeds, blankets, and oriental rugs will go too. I already packed all the crystal and silverware as well as paintings and jewelry. Father emptied his bookcases of valuable books. From now on we have to sleep on these straw mattresses that the Red Cross brought us this morning."

I was stunned. I had intended to tell Mother of my good grades in English and Biology and how I had been asked to read the poem I had written in German class. But all this was not important now.

Mother hugged me and assured me that our goods would be much safer in the country. Bombs had seldom fallen there.

The truck did not arrive that day. Instead it came when I was in school the next day. When I came home everything was gone. The house was empty, the floors bare. The straw mattresses were hard and bumpy, but at least Mother had kept our feather pillows.

Now it was 1945, the war had ended. We had not seen our household goods in two years. There was no way of communication available. We had no mail, no newspaper, no phone, no trains, no cars. No travel was allowed. The country was divided in zones. We now lived in the French zone. It was a temporary arrangement until the Allied Forces made permanent plans.

We had curfew hours from sundown to sunup. Jeeps with French soldiers patrolled the streets. Machine-guns were mounted on their jeeps and anyone found on the streets during curfew was shot. A friend of ours, a young mother whose child had gotten very ill during the night tried to run to the hospital, but she and her little boy were shot to death.

"How and when will we ever be able to find out any news about our evacuated household goods. The war is over, but we do not know if everything was stolen, destroyed or is still in that church basement." Mother was desperate. She wanted to finally get the house back to the comforts we had known before the war. She was tired of "living like gypsies," as she called it.

Father had a good idea. He had a permit and a motorcycle. He would drive to the French border, show his pass and surely would be let through. He wanted to take me along, wearing a Red Cross armband, pretending I was a nurse. He had a big Red Cross painted on the front fender of the heavy motorcycle. Surely, the French soldiers would be impressed by such an official looking duo. But there was this one problem—I had no permit to cross. Father said he would take care of this when the need arose.

And anyway, we had been assured by some well experienced border crossers, "If you come very early in the morning—especially on a rainy day—the borders will be unguarded. You simply push your vehicle along the side of the barrier." It sounded simple enough.

Father picked a rainy night to decide that he and I would rise at five and get to the border by six. It would still be raining. We would turn off the motor and quietly slip through. That was the plan, a very sensible and "doable" plan, so we thought.

The next morning we arrived at the border before daybreak and, yes, it was still raining. We must have been practically invisible as we stopped and proceeded with The Plan. We did not speak, we just quietly pushed the bike.

Suddenly, there he stood, in his plastic American-made olive green poncho, dripping wet. "Permit and reason for crossing," the Frenchman was precise.

Neither Father nor I knew enough French to explain. Father spoke loud and slow in German. "Here is my pass. Here is my ID card. I have the permission to look after a hospital and some church property."

The guard took Father's documents, which were correct. Then the guard looked at me. "Where are your papers?"

I shrugged and pretended not to understand. I handed him my ID card. He shook his head.

"That's not enough. Where is your pass?"

I had none.

Father tried to explain that I was his daughter helping him on this important trip.

It was daylight now. The rain had stopped. We stood in front of the red-blue-white-striped barrier. The guard did not want to let us through. Some more French soldiers appeared. They had shouldered their rifles and were ready for the day's activities.

All the guards now huddled together and studied Father's papers. They looked at him then at me. They mumbled in

French and occasionally laughed out loud. What were they talking about? Why didn't they just open that barrier and let us through?

Finally one soldier announced, pointing to Father. "You may go, but your daughter may not." The guard gave Father back his documents.

"That is impossible. We are here in the middle of the Black Forest, no town in sight. We are fifty miles from home. You must let her get through." Father insisted.

The other fellows came closer. One said, "Mademoiselle, you stay here and peel potatoes for our dinner until your father comes back."

They all laughed. They thought this to be a big joke. "Or your father pays us one hundred Marks ($50) and you may go with him."

No responsible father would leave his sixteen-year-old daughter in the hands of a group of wild-eyed foreign troops. Peel Potatoes, yes sure . . .

Father always carried a lot of cash. He had learned to bribe people if this became necessary. He quickly pulled out a One-Hundred-Mark note and we were on our way. We drove straight to the village where our goods were stored.

Although we saw many French troops on the way, we arrived at the little church with no trouble. We parked the motorbike behind the fence and talked to the minister, Rev. Mueller. He had just recently been released from an American prisoner of war camp nearby. It was so strange hearing reports of men who were rounded up as prisoners of war in their own country.

"We were kept in an open field surrounded by rolls of barbed wire for six months. The rain soaked this field many times and many of the men became ill with pneumonia. Some very sick ones were released early," Rev. Mueller told us.

He also told us that during his absence refugees had moved into the church. They had found our stored goods in the church cellar and, of course, had started to use them. We found our Persian rugs spread out on the basement floor, our mattresses and featherbeds, as well as our beautiful camel hair blankets in obvious use on the cellar floor. We found our good china and silver in the kitchen sink. I did not like what I saw. The refugees were nowhere in sight.

Father was sympathetic, "These people were driven from their homeland and lost everything. Temporarily they will use our goods, but as soon as possible we will get everything back."

This was easier said than done. For another year we lived "like gypsies," as Mother called it. Then, one by one the tracks were repaired and trains started to roll again. We each had a new ID card, since we were now in the American zone. We were allowed to travel to the other Western zones—British and French—without too much hassle. The Russian zone, East Germany, had become part of the Soviet Union and was closed to West Germans. The Iron Curtain went right through our country.

I remember vividly the first train trip Mother and I took to retrieve our jewelry and silverware. Mother and I each carried an empty duffle bag. The train arrived in the little town and I was able to show Mother the way to the church. Oh, yes, I remembered the way! A year before Father and I had the adventure with the motorcycle and the French guards who wanted to keep me in their mess hall to peel potatoes.

Much of the silverware was in the sink with some unwashed dishes. I cleaned and dried everything, while Mother talked to the refugee family. They thanked us for letting them use our housewares. We understood. We shook hands and left with the understanding that sooner or later the furniture would be picked up by truck. They nodded.

We wrapped the silverware in pillowcases before carefully placing the bundles in our duffle bags. I lifted mine.

"Oh, my goodness, I had no idea it would be that heavy. How will I ever carry that bag all the way to the train station."

Luckily, we had allowed an hour to walk that mile to the station. Mother and I made many stops, put down the heavy bags, stretched our tired arms, rested a moment and then walked on.

A young man offered to carry my heavy load, but I would

not let go of my valuable treasure. He might have taken the bag and run away with our silver. I did not want to risk it, after all it had survived the war and use by honest refugees. Not a piece was missing.

Now I worried about the French troops, guarding the train station. They had the right to make me open the bag and they could have confiscated everything in it.

But I acted quite nonchalantly. I climbed on the train after Mother and found a seat. I put my bag on my lap and covered it with my jacket.

The wooden benches were hard, the old steam engine puffed out the smoke. The window was open because it was a hot day. The soot settled in my tired eyes. I closed them and dozed until we stopped in Stuttgart.

We carried our duffle bags home. It was a half hour walk up the hill, but we made it at last. Mother and I were overjoyed, and so was the rest of the family. Our lives were getting better! At least we had our good silver back.

Later that year the hospital truck stopped and delivered the rest of our furniture. What luxury! We had our bedding back. The Red Cross was glad to pick up the old straw mattresses. There were still plenty of refugees who had to sleep on bare floors till now.

The only treasures that had been stolen were Mother's jewelry, including an old fashioned garnet necklace that had belonged to Oma, Mother's mom. It was irreplaceable but not important anymore.

Thunder Over the Mountains

This is the nursery rhyme I learned in preschool, before the war. It was my favorite "finger play" because we children were encouraged to make the appropriate noises with our hands and feet.

"Raindrops are falling ever so gently.
The raindrops get louder and stronger.
Now it pours and pours. There is lightning.
There's thunder, loud thunder. There's hail.
All the people run home."

At the beginning of the poem we gently let our fingers fall onto the table tops. Then faster and louder.

"There's lightning . . ." we stretched out our arms and let them zigzag down while making a hissing noise. "There's thunder . . ." as loudly as we could we drummed our fists on the table and also stamped our feet. Our knuckles knocked. "There's hail." "All the people run home." Two fingers on each hand became the running feet that ended behind our backs. All quiet.

Several years later our family spent a summer holiday in the Bavarian Alps. "How beautiful . . . for mountains majesty." This was the first time my sisters and I saw the really high mountains. Before that we had visited the hills around Stuttgart, higher ones in the Black Forest and the Jurassic Mountains, but the Alps were by far the most awesome.

Grey granite rocks with white snow caps now looked down on us. Narrow paths took us higher and higher towards the peaks. The spectacular view from the mountain tops was breathtaking. The tree line was far below. Up here grew only short-needled shrubs.

Tiny villages lay far below. Even the cattle, grazing on mountain meadows, seemed like tiny toy figurines. Only the pleasant ringing of their bells around their necks reminded us of them being real live creatures.

"Do you see that?" Father wanted to make sure we observed nature properly. "Whenever the cows stretch their necks to reach for a tasty mouthful of grass or herbs, their bells ring. Do you hear the 'ring-a-ling' of the calves' tiny bells? The farmers can tell where their animals are grazing by this lovely sound. No cow or calf can get lost."

We listened attentively, and Father was pleased. Occasionally we heard a "moo, moo." I loved the peaceful sounds of the mountains.

"Yoo-hooh, yoo-hoo." Father yodeled in his deep voice and dozens of echoes returned from the steep, rocky mountains around us.

"I want to try, too." I yodeled my name as loudly as I could. And sure enough, the echo came back. "Gudrun, Gudrun, Gudrun," each echo softer than the previous one.

Now my sisters joined in with their names. What fun this was. The mountains seemed to speak to us personally as we heard our names repeated over and over. "Siglinde, Siglinde." Then "Christa, Christa."

Suddenly the sun disappeared. It became cool and windy. Within minutes the clouds covered the mountain tops and sank down to the valley, covering everything with a grey, opaque veil.

We tried to outrun the clouds. We had left our raincoats back in the hotel. We knew that soon the rain would start. We ran as fast as our legs would carry us down the path.

Finally we arrived at the forest of beech and oak trees in the valley. We searched for shelter from the storm, and the tree branches looked to us like live umbrellas. What a relief!

Lightning hissed past us, thunder echoed from the mountains above. I was reminded of a proverb: "In a thunderstorm avoid the oaks but seek shelter under a beech tree." Oaks attract lightning. I knew that. We kept running until we finally reached a young beech.

"I am soaking wet," Christa complained. We all were. Our jackets were pulled over our heads but the rain poured right through.

"It's only rain, we'll get dry again." Father's soothing voice consoled his drenched daughters.

We huddled together under the tree dripping and shivering with fear and cold. I covered my ears with my hands. I was afraid of the thunder.

At last the rain let up, the thunder echoed from a distance. We looked at each other and laughed. "We all look like wet mice."

Yes, we certainly did.

The summer storm had come and gone quickly. By the time we arrived at the hotel, the warm sun had almost dried our hair and clothes. Mother was glad to see us safe and sound. She was worried about us.

"In the future, please remember to take your raincoats when climbing a mountain. Even if the sun shines as you leave."

We took Mother's advice seriously. Having changed to dry clothes we now sipped hot chocolate on the hotel patio and again listened to the peaceful sounds of the cow bells. This day had been an adventure to remember.

That had been peace time. But now it was war. War was

intruding into our very lives. Death and destruction hung like black, dangerous clouds over us. Lightning-like flashes of falling bombs ripped the night skies. Thunderous explosions and artillery pierced the air. Fiery phosphorus and hot ashes rained on us.

"Why, Lord, why?" I did not understand. No more restful night, no peaceful sleep. I was so tired of living in constant danger. "Oh, if only I could die."

But the war ended and summer again warmed the country side. The sights and smells of death and destruction were still with us. But, oh wonder, we could now sleep at night. What a blessing. "Thank you, Lord, thank you for peace in our land."

August 1945

I lay peacefully sleeping on my straw mattress. We had not been able to get back our bedding and other goods we had evacuated to the country side during the war. My sheet was tightly wrapped around me and I was dreaming.

During the night thunderclouds had gathered. Suddenly, a roll of thunder had crashed nearby. I jumped up from my deep sleep. I could barely open my eyes. Instinctively I grabbed my clothes, slipped on my shoes and ran for the door. Another roll of thunder. Christa had also been awakened. She rubbed her eyes and looked at me, puzzled.

"What are you doing? Why are you dressed?"

"Oh, Christa, get up quickly. Didn't you hear the falling bombs?"

"This is only thunder." My sister tried to comfort me. "Remember, the war is over."

I was now fully awake. Another roll of thunder. Yes, now I remembered. The war was over. No more bombs, no more running to the shelter. Thank God. I sank back into my bed. Thunder never frightened me again.

"Good night, Christa," I whispered as I cuddled up to my camel hair blanket. "Good night, Gudrun," Christa was already half asleep.

Foreign Military Occupation: French

From one day to the next Stuttgart became an occupied city. For us the war ended with the Lost Battle of Stuttgart. For two hellish days and nights the fighting lasted.

The city fathers had surrendered in the evening of April 21, 1945, but to the east of us the fierce battles raged on. We still heard the bombers flying overhead, the constant thunder of artillery and explosions of bombs still shook the earth and the city still had to be kept in total darkness at night.

Before surrendering to the French and Senegalese (troops lead by General Charles De Gaulle) our city government was able to function in some fashion. We still had radio and newspapers to inform us of the progress of the war.

All this ended. The German troops either surrendered to the enemy or retreated towards the east where the fighting continued. Occupying foreign troops now roamed the streets, plundering, killing, raping.

My sisters and I were fourteen, sixteen, and eighteen years old. Our whole childhood and youth had been spent in war and its aftermath. And now we had to worry about being raped by these enemy troops from Africa, who were so foreign and whose language we did not understand!

We did not dare leaving the house without our parents. When we saw some soldiers stumbling drunk on one side of the street we quickly ran to the opposite side walk or hid behind a garden gate or in a ruin. I remember seeing an old man being pulled out of his house, beaten unmercifully with rifles, then forced to eat bags of salt until he collapsed and died.

Herr Benz, next door, was found dead. He had been such a good neighbor. But he was a Party member and so was hanged in his basement. Miss Hummel, one of our teachers was raped by six soldiers and died. Every day brought new atrocities.

One day I saw a jeep full of Senegalese troops, their arms totally covered with stolen wrist watches, their fingers sparkling with precious rings, all was stolen from civilians.

One day a big military truck stopped at the hospital. French troops rounded up all men: Father, Dr. Neuffer, Dr. Nase, Dr. Port, the janitor and even some patients. They pushed them all onto the truck and without explanation took them away. They were gone all day. It was getting dark and we had not heard from the men. Mother, my sisters, and I stayed at the hospital during the night. We kept looking out for Father, we worried about him and the other men.

Finally, the next morning Father returned.

"My goodness, what happened to you, Dad?" We were all shocked to see Father.

"You look awful, your suit is black with soot, your shirt is torn."

Father was always impeccably dressed, and now this.

"Sit here, next to me and I will tell you what happened."

We all sat down on the stone steps of the hospital entrance and Father began to speak. His voice sounded desperate and almost hopeless.

"We German people are now at the mercy of the enemy

troops. We have no rights, no laws to protect us. We used to lead such ordered lives, now their is only chaos."

"But why are you so dirty, Daddy, where did they take you?" I wanted to hear his story.

"Well," continued Father, "After they found more men and loaded them all onto the truck, the troops took us to an abandoned coal yard way over in the Western part of the city. They made us stand up all day with rows of other men they had brought to this place. One by one our shirts were ripped open and the soldiers, apparently, looked for something.

"One soldier finally pushed a man to the side, hit him with his rifle and yelled in broken German, 'You SS-man, you criminal, you die.'

"Apparently the soldier had found the SS-tatoo under the man's right arm. Now we all knew what this search was about. They wanted to find members of the SS, Hitler's security guards."

Of course Father was no Party man or member of any Nazi-organization. After the soldiers had searched him and found no tatoo, they pushed him over to the side of the innocents, but they still were kept until morning. After many hours of standing they had been allowed to sit on a heap of coal.

"That is why I look so dirty. The wind blew coal dust in our faces all night long. The thing that worries me the most is that I do not know what happened to the other men from the hospital. I suspect that Dr. Port was a member of the SS, but I am not sure."

As we looked up, we saw Herr Vollmer, the janitor walking up the driveway. They had let him go, too. It had taken him, like Father, two hours to walk back from the coal yard through the ruins of Stuttgart and we were all glad to see him.

Eventually the other men returned one by one, but not Dr. Port. Father was later notified that Dr. Port had been a member of the SS, and he was imprisoned in a French concentration camp. We felt sorry for his wife and four young children. Their home was confiscated and they moved to live with relatives.

It was years before Dr. Port was released. He was totally

emaciated and very ill. He never practiced medicine again and died young.

By the middle of May, on a Sunday, we dared to leave the house and take a walk downtown to see what was going on. I really did not want to go, but Father encouraged me. "We'll be all right as long as we stay together."

The city was in ruins. The rubble covered roads and sidewalks. It was hard to find our way to the City Center. The Castle Square was full of enemy tanks and soldiers. We saw friends and stopped to talk to them. We were so glad to see that, like ourselves, they were survivors. But just then a French soldier with a riding-whip came up to us and yelled. "You are not allowed to congregate, walk on, now!" And with that he swung his whip at us. I quickly ducked and we all ran in different directions.

We returned home as quickly as we could and did not go downtown again for a long time.

One day it was announced that the French Military Government made known by flyers that a complete set of men's clothing must be brought to the Jakob School, a now closed elementary school. Those people who had been Nazi Party members also would have to deliver mattresses, bed linens, and pillows. This was supposed to be part of the "Reparations" that the German people owed France. The set of clothing included a suit, sweater, hat, raincoat, shoes, socks, and underclothing. What a terrible thing. Our men had not been able to buy new clothes for years!

Father had only three suits left. Two were black winter outfits and one was a light grey summer suit. Father also had a club foot. He was born that way. Although this did not hinder his walking, he had to wear hand knitted socks, one much smaller than the other as well as custom-made shoes.

Mother fixed up a bundle of Father's clothes without shoes and socks. When I arrived at the school a long line of frightened people stood and waited for the doors to open. French soldiers stood guard. Finally we were let in. To my great shock I found that a German woman, watched by French soldiers with guns, was accepting the clothes.

"You traitor," I thought angrily.

I opened my carefully wrapped bundle and the woman looked through everything.

"Socks and shoes are missing. I cannot accept this," she said coldly.

"Father has to wear custom made shoes and socks," I tried to explain.

"You have to bring me proof of this," was her reply.

I had to give her our name and address. She shoved the clothes towards me. I had to wrap them up and take them back with me. Luckily, Father's orthopedic shoemaker, Herr Kuolt, lived near the hospital where he also had his workshop. I stopped there.

Oh, yes, he would be glad to write me a note to explain Father's crippled foot. Thanking him for his kindness I trotted back to the Jakob School and was finally able to satisfy the *enemy's* demands.

I wondered what on Earth possessed them to do this. All the delivered clothes had been thrown on a big pile on the school's gymnasium floor. "That's what we get for losing the war," I mumbled angrily.

The French Occupation lasted until late summer of 1945. Then we became part of the American zone. Thank goodness.

These two men became the chief and vice chief of the U.S. military government for the city of Stuttgart in 1945.

American Military Occupation

A few days after De Gaulle's troops had occupied our city, an American officer with his entourage walked from house to house in our neighborhood. They checked to see which of the homes could be used for U.S. troops for Rest and Recreation. These troops would move on after a week or two.

The U.S. officer and group of soldiers with their rifles did not need the permission of the homeowners to walk through their houses, open armoir, pulling out linens, or open cupboards. We did not know what they were looking for, but Father had heard that our neighborhood would become American.

Sure enough, the next day all homes had to evacuate, and the soldiers moved in. Our house was spared because Father had an impressively large sign put up bearing a Red Cross and several signatures and stamps.

All other homeowners had to leave within two hours of the notice, some stayed with us. Every morning, while the troops lined up in front of our house for roll call, the homeowners had to clean up after the soldiers and do their laundry. Their shirts had to be ironed a certain way with pleats in exactly the right places. Our flag pole, high up on our garden wall, was visible through the whole neighborhood. There was no better place to hoist the American flag than on our pole. Hiding behind a curtain we girls watched and listened.

A dark haired American soldier blew his trumpet from our garden wall every morning and evening, and two others unfolded and hoisted the Stars and Stripes. We could hardly believe that this was reality. It seemed impossible to see an enemy flag on our pole, where a few weeks earlier our German flag was flying.

One night two American soldiers came to our front door and demanded to be let in. Mother pretended not to understand, but when the soldiers pointed their guns at her, she had to open the door. They went straight to the living room, where our beautiful Telefunken radio stood. They unplugged it and took it away.

A week later we heard a commotion outside during the night. The language was American. The roaring of vehicles, shouting, and yelling had awakened us. We stayed away from the windows. Electricity was still turned off during the night, because the war was still going on to our east. The next morning all was quiet. The troops had left taking many things with them as "souvenirs." Our radio was gone too.

Summer 1945. (From my diary)
Stuttgart will become American, the zones have been redrawn. Karlsruhe (to the west of us), occupied by Americans at the end of the war now became French. It was traded for Stuttgart.

We were relieved. Signs now announced "American Zone." We had heard that treatment by U.S. soldiers was much more humane.

It happened that the same troops from the 100th Infantry Division, 397th Regiment who had occupied our neighborhood in Spring were back. We were glad to see them and we recognized them at once. The same dark haired soldier was back with his trumpet, and he still made the same mistake when he blew TAPS. Father had left the Red Cross sign on the garden gate, and again we were spared. The German homeowners on our street again had to move out and clean up after the soldiers in the mornings.

We wondered what had happened to our radio. Then one morning architect Mueller's wife came over and told Mother, "I saw a Telefunken radio in my house. It does not belong to me. There are other things the soldiers brought with them. I do not know where they took them. But the radio may be yours. It has two water spots on top."

Mother was encouraged. "Oh, yes, I always had two Japanese vases with flowers on top of the radio, which left some water spots. I wish I could go with you and see for myself."

The two ladies whispered something. Obviously they had a plan. The next morning while the soldiers were assembled as usual for their morning drill, Mother and Frau Mueller quietly slipped in the back door. Sure enough, Mother recognized our radio. Luckily she had filed away the brochure and serial number from the day of purchase. She had heard from other neighbors that if one could prove ownership of items taken by the troops, one may be lucky enough to get them back.

Mother, brochure in hand, bravely marched to the officer in charge. Within a very short time the radio had to be returned, and the same soldier who had taken it earlier in the year had to place it back on its former stand. It was a miracle to us. Now at least we could listen to news on the one station operating under U.S. Military Control.

Wealthy Frau Bauer's Villa was made into a mess hall. Frau Bauer was an old lady who always sat in her glassed-in sun room with her caged parrot. I waved at her whenever I passed her house. She smiled back. Now she had to leave her beautiful home to occupying troops. We never saw her again. All soldiers ate in that lovely mansion, at least 150 men.

For us German people electricity was still limited to two

hours in the morning and from seven to nine o'clock at night. The U.S. troops were not affected by this rule. They burned lights day and night, even when they were not inside. We thought this to be a terrible waste.

After a few weeks we girls lost some of our fears and ventured out of the house. By then the troops were allowed contact with the civilians and we were eager to try our English. We had studied British Queen's English all through the war but never had any opportunity to use it in conversation. It was, however, sometimes difficult to understand the Americans. They seemed to talk too fast and often used different pronunciations from what we had learned. But after a while we became used to it.

One of the first things the soldiers asked us was, "Is your father or other relative a Nazi."

"No," was our short answer.

One day I sat on our balcony mending some socks. Across the street a soldier whistled at me to get my attention.

"Hey cutie, would you like this orange?"

He held up a beautiful ripe fruit. We had not seen oranges in years and I nodded "yes." But when he actually came running up our steps and rang the door bell, I was frightened.

"Mother, please answer the door, a soldier wants to give me an orange," I whispered anxiously.

Mother opened the little glass window in the front door and gratefully received the orange.

"Oh, ja. Thank you very much," she tried her limited English.

We all gathered around and held and smelled the lovely fruit.

"It may be poisoned, I don't know if we should eat it," was my worry.

But it looks perfectly fine," said Christa. "Let's peel it and try just one little slice."

We ate the whole orange, and it tasted heavenly.

This small deed of kindness was the bridge between two countries which had been deadly enemies just a few months earlier. It was not long after that when we brought out our tennis rackets and balls, strung a rope across the street and played. American soldiers on one side, German girls on the other. Tennis courts had not been opened to the Germans. Only the U.S. officers were allowed to use them.

One red-haired soldier showed me a picture of his pretty wife and children. He was homesick for them and hoped to soon return to the USA. His name was Jack and he called me Mildred, because, he said, I reminded him of his wife who also had dark hair and blue eyes. Jack was older than the rest. Most were barely out of their teens.

Charles was the fellow who gave me the orange. Father once asked him for some gasoline. A motorcycle had been issued Father, but white German gas was very hard to find. Only one small gas station was open. American gasoline was orange in color and available on the Black Market. Sometimes vehicles were stopped and the contents of their tanks checked. If orange gas was found, the vehicle was confiscated at once.

Charles gave him a bucketful of American gasoline. Father really took a chance, but he desperately needed to drive to Ulm and look after the hospital there, as well as the Old Peoples' Home. Father made it to Ulm and back safely. Thank goodness nobody checked his gas tank.

These American boys really did not have enough to do. They took off in their jeeps from time to time to patrol the area or to go to the mess hall. Other times they sat on the curb and watched the girls. They had learned one German phrase they repeated every time a young woman passed by.

"Hey, Fraulein, wohin gehen Sie?" ("Hey, Miss, where are you going?")

U.S. soldiers had three items that were irresistible to Germans. They had chocolate, chewing gum, and cigarettes (Lucky Strikes, Camels, and Chesterfields). These items could be traded for any favor. I was quite disgusted to see a German man actually picking up a soldier's cigarette butts from the street and smoking them. Yes, these were hard times and many people lost their sense of national and personal pride.

I watched some soldiers having fun with this. One of them tied a cigarette butt to a string, placed it on the sidewalk, sat on the windowsill, and held the string in his hand. When a man bent down to pick up the butt, this guy pulled on the string and dangled the cigarette butt in front of the man always just out of reach. The soldiers laughed as hard as they could. The man walked on.

How humiliating, I thought.

That summer we had "double daylight savings time." Why? Because we had to be on Moscow time. We did not understand. We knew that the four victorious Allies were America, England, France, and the Soviet Union. But we lived in the West. We could understand why the Russian zone of Germany would have Moscow time, but why would we? That question was never answered. After all we were living under foreign rule and had to live by their laws. That summer daylight lasted until midnight; curfew was 10:00 p.m. to 6:00 a.m.

Every so often, the soldiers had to clean their guns. They sat on the benches in the little park across the street from our house. I was surprised to see them using gasoline to do this job. They poured the gas into their helmets and held them between their knees. Once a soldier flicked his burning cigarette into the gas-filled helmet of a comrade. Flash, a huge flame shot up, burned the soldiers hair and hands, started a fire up in some trees, and sent everyone running.

One day a military truck arrived and a beautiful dapple-grey horse was unloaded. The soldiers let the horse roam in some neighborhood yards and occasionally one of them would ride him. I have no idea where this horse came from. Apparently it had been stolen from a riding-school.

Finally, after seven weeks of occupying our neighborhood, the troops were transferred to former German military barracks in another part of town.

Jack and Paul, a very young soldier from West Virginia, had tears in their eyes. They left around noon. We waved good-bye. Mother did not think that was necessary, after all they were enemy troops. Slowly our neighborhood again became a quiet street where everyone had returned to their homes and tried to repair war damages and find misplaced items due to the seven weeks of foreign occupation.

Frau Schatzmann found paintings and crystal that did not belong to her. Others found photo albums and jewelry. People had to go from house to house and search for their missing belongings. Many items were found; others had become souvenirs for the soldiers.

Frau Reichard, the piano teacher across from us, lamented that the case of her grand piano had been hacked to pieces and the wood used for a cozy fire one cool evening.

Applecake and Hot Chocolate
or The Peace Party

I sat on the balcony and mended my silk stocking. It was a pleasant summer day in our now quiet neighborhood. The U.S. troops had left together with all their noisy music and roaring vehicles. It took a steady hand to pick up that tiny stitch that had caused the long run on my stocking.

"There, I got you," I triumphantly stuck my fine-hooked needle into the elusive, tiny loop and—row after row—I hooked the stitch all the way to the top of the stocking. The run was repaired. I used one of my long brown hairs to fasten the last loop to the rest of the stocking.

I held it up to check my masterpiece. Yes, it was perfect. I could not even tell there ever was a run in that silk stocking. I was pleased with myself and the world. Tomorrow was Sunday and I had good stockings.

A noisy U.S. vehicle roaring up the street brought me back to reality. I looked down from the balcony and to my horror a jeep had stopped in front of our house and four servicemen jumped out, came running up our stairs, rang the door bell.

"Oh no, the American soldiers are back. What are we going to do? Will they again occupy our neighborhood or confiscate some of our belongings?"

I was in panic and ran to tell Mother.

"Well," said Mother, "Let's answer the door and find out what they want."

She opened the little glass window in the front door. "Oh ja, hallo," she wanted to appear calm and friendly. "So, you are back." Mother recognized the four men. I hid behind her but was curious.

This unexpected visit was during a time when an intense hunt for Nazis had started. Most of the Party members were harmless citizens who had joined Hitler's party in order to keep their jobs. But we saw many of our neighbors being hauled away to be interrogated by U.S. Military Courts. The years of Denazification had begun.

Anyone who was arrested was "guilty until proven innocent." Father had been asked by several neighbors to testify in their favor. After Father had proven his own innocence he could then help others.

When I saw the soldiers, all these thoughts flashed before me. Were they going to take Father away? What would happen next? Father never talked about his experiences with the American High Command.

When Mother saw a box of food being carried by one of the soldiers, she opened the door.

"Ah, ja, hallo Harold." She had recognized one of the soldiers, a captain in his splendid uniform. Harold spoke German. His parents had emigrated to the States a generation ago.

Harold handed Mother the box. "Here," he said simply. "Next Saturday evening at eight o'clock I will come here with twelve friends. Bake us a big apfelkuchent and make cocoa to go with it. Everything you will need is in the box, except apples."

Mother was speechless, but nodded in agreement.

The soldiers left. Mother carried the box to the kitchen. Let's see. Yes, there was flour, sugar, shortening, dried eggs, dried milk and Hershey's Cocoa.

"I guess, Harold is homesick for some good German baking." I believe Mother, deep down, was pleased to be asked this favor. Harold could have been her son.

We all sat down and thought about Saturday night and how we would handle Harold's order to host such a party.

Father came in and we told him the exciting story. He was not amused. "I will tell you right now about one thing that is not going to happen Saturday night. This party will not be held in this house. No matter what the Americans demand ,they are not going to put a foot in this place. Period. No 'ifs' or 'buts,' please!" Father had spoken, his word was command.

We were not going to "collaborate with the enemy."

Wednesday, Thursday, Friday passed. We all worried about the party, but no one had a good idea.

Late Friday night Mother offered a solution. She had planned it all week, now it was time to reveal The Plan.

Mother had spoken with Frau Lohr across the street. Frau Lohr had a beautiful garden and patio and she agreed to host an outdoor party. Mother was going to take care of the cake, Frau Lohr agreed to make cocoa. She invited a few neighbor ladies and their children to make decorations. We were going to make this a Fest to Remember. Several of our young friends were invited. The weather cooperated beautifully and Mother found the huge baking sheet with handles on each end. This antique had been stored away in the attic. Now it was useful.

The problem was this. We had a gas stove, but gas was rationed. We could only use it sparingly. No way could we bake several cakes for this expected crowd without risking the penalty of having our gas turned off for a month.

Baker Mauser had agreed to bake this huge apple cake for us. We girls peeled, cored, and sliced apples all Saturday morning. The apples came from our own garden.

Mother mixed, worked, rolled several batches of dough, and spread it. The baking sheet had been our salvation. In former times it had been used for bread-baking in the country where farmers baked several loaves at one time. Two people had to carry the unbaked loaves to the bake-house where the baker took care of each family's initialed baking sheets.

The apples had to be placed in perfectly straight rows. Mother oversaw, and I performed this job well. Then Christa and I were chosen to carry the cake to the bakery. We walked carefully down the hill. It was a ten minute walk. The cloth covering the cake had to be held down with one hand. We took turns with this difficult task. The wind tried to lift the cloth for all the world to see our masterpiece. It did not succeed.

"So, you are going to have company," Herr Mauser smiled as he put the cake in his huge brick oven. "Come back in an hour or so. By then it will be somewhat cooled."

We did.

In the meantime the Lohr's garden was transformed into a lovely, colorful piece of paradise. The neighbor ladies had decorated the clothesline with paper lampions. Everyone had donated candle stumps. This was going to be a well lighted party. The street lights had not been turned on, so the whole city was still as pitch black at night as it had been during the war. Electricity was still rationed. We were allowed to use it from eight to ten in the morning, and from seven to ten at night.

I made little place cards using pressed flowers, and we spread rose petals all over the table centers. A few minutes before eight, Christa and I took big platters of apfelkuchen across the street and placed them on the decorated tables.

"Remember, curfew is at ten o'clock. You must be home before then," Mother reminded us.

Three jeeps with soldiers arrived. We were excited and fearful at the same time. Would the men like what we had prepared for them? Would it be good enough for these rich Americans?

There was Paul and Jack, Harold and Charles, along with some fellows we did not know.

They seemed surprised to see the beauty of the candle-lit garden. They were much quieter than before when they had been our occupying forces, much more civil.

We ate and drank and somehow conversed in part English, part German. The bright full moon smiled down on us. The night was warm and so was the feeling of friendship.

For the first time I realized the meaning of "world citizen." We were brothers and sisters that evening. I had never hated the "enemy," this faceless, nameless thing that dropped firebombs and explosives on us. Politically incorrect? Perhaps.

It suddenly became clear to me that these men we had entertained this evening were ordinary human beings, with hopes and fears like ours. Like us they had been thrown into the most terrifying war without their say-so. They had also seen death around them. They, like we, had huddled in bunkers and prayed for survival. Those experiences we had in common even though we had lived through war on opposite sides.

The difference was that these soldiers had been on the winning side. They would receive medals for their deeds. They could leave the destroyed cities behind and return to their rich country. They could continue their education and go back to a normal life. We were stuck here.

"If only I could visit America one day," I sighed.

Shortly after ten o'clock, Mother appeared. She was worried about us. Christa and I had enjoyed such a good time, we had forgotten all about curfew and foreign occupation troops.

A military patrol jeep with mounted machine-guns slowed down to inspect the party. But when they saw the Americans in uniform they slowly drove on.

Do these young Americans remember that warm summer evening in 1945, when we ate apfelkuchen together and drank cocoa in a candle-lit garden? Would they tell their children about it? We do not know. After that evening we never saw them again.

Without having made a conscious effort we had celebrated peace. It would not have been possible a few months earlier when we were still regarding each other as enemies. A Peace Party, how unforgettable.

Hunger

Lack of needed nourishment to sustain life does strange things to all living creatures. Hunger affects our whole selves—body, soul, and mind. It keeps us from thinking clearly. It dulls our feelings of compassion for others. It makes us selfish and suspicious, weak, and tired.

During the first eight years of Hitler's reign the country had plenty of everything we needed. No one was hungry, the government made sure of that. We could not imagine not having an abundance of food and having to cope with hunger. But war and its long aftermath caused this misery. Rich or poor, we all had to suffer.

Usually the military will receive the largest portions of available food. The civilian population not only has to cope with the destruction of their homes, workplaces, churches, and schools, but also has to find ways to prevent starvation.

This is an especially difficult task in cities where most

people live in apartments and have no way of growing some of their own food. Surely, here and there little plots of vegetables spring up, and they are jealously guarded from would-be thieves. They are sometimes even found on balconies in flower pots. We grew beautiful green beans on our balcony, good for one or two meals. That was all.

During World War II, as a child, I remember how I relished reaching for green, very sour gooseberries through the slats of a garden fence on my way to school. These berries pucker up one's mouth when they are still green. Besides that they give one a terrible stomach ache. But the temptation was so great, I disregarded all consequences. I also recall the big cherry, apple, and peach trees whose branches shaded the sidewalks and whose fallen, often bruised fruits were gladly picked up by hungry passersby.

In addition I always had my eyes on the wild hazelnut trees. In fall their fruits covered the sidewalks and I always came home with a pocketful of them. I sat on our garden steps and crushed them with my heel. They usually ended up being smashed to small pieces, but this did not keep me from patiently picking them from the shell and enjoying their sweet crunchy meat.

For a long time after the war we ate potato soup and a piece of heavy black bread. Every night it was the same meal: soup and bread. The bakers had to use potatoes along with the rye flour. They were not allowed to sell the bread on the day it was baked. It had to be at least two days old. Even then it was too heavy to eat. We had to wait another three days before we cut it with our slicing machine.

I believe it is the lack of certain minerals and vitamins that drove us to eat all kinds of strange wild growing plants, nuts, and fruits. Nettles became a substitute for spinach. We also gathered wild anise and caraway seeds. Camomile and mint were picked for tea. When we walked along country roads we always had our eyes open to discover edible plants.

Before the war ended, my parents were able to buy a beautiful piece of land with a wonderful view of orchards, villages, hills, and dales. It had been a vineyard for over one hundred years, but now the whole hillside was terraced and planted with over one hundred and ten trees and shrubs. It was my parents' dream to built their retirement home there after the war.

This land was about ten or twelve miles out of Stuttgart. It was difficult to harvest all that fruit and transport it home to our cellar, but it certainly was a Godsend during those difficult years.

When one owned such a valuable piece of land, one was obliged to report the amount of fruit harvested. The local authorities sent crews who picked berries, apples, pears, and walnuts and took them to a co-op. Father, however, gave most of it to the hospital. We also supplied friends and neighbors.

Our green grocer went to market twice a week in his pick-up truck. We began to stand in line long before he returned from market. Whatever he was able to purchase wholesale, whether salad, carrots or potatoes, we were there, eager to buy his wares.

An hour later his store was empty and closed.

After the war, during French occupation it was hard to get anything from the butchershop. The French troops confiscated all meat from the farmers. The German population was only able to purchase blood sausage or innards like heart, kidney, liver, brain or tripe (cow's stomach). We had never eaten these parts before. It was most humbling.

We had boxes of money but could not even buy decent food. During the war everything was well organized and on Sundays we even had a small roast or some frankfurters. After the war, however, times became really desperate. Yet we found the truth in the saying, "Need breeds invention," and somehow we were able to prepare halfway tasty dishes.

Getting salt was another problem. Only grey salt could be purchased. That was the way it came from the mine. It had dirt, small rocks, and sand mixed in. It was up to us to find ways to clean and purify the salt. So we did the sensible thing. We boiled it covered with water.

The salt dissolved, we strained the brew carefully, leaving the dirt and rocks behind in the pot. Then followed the time-consuming task of boiling the saltwater down until all moisture had evaporated, and there it was, almost white salt.

The French troops celebrated their victory over Germany during the night of May 8, 1945. Instead of fireworks they used all U.S. ammunition and shot it in the air. We had never heard such roar of artillery, machine-gun fire, exploding bombs, and other weapons as we did that night after Germany surrendered unconditionally to the Allied Forces.

Then the French and Senegalese troops went through the city in a rampage to find wine and other alcohol. When doing so, they came across the wine cellar in the Old Castle in the center of the city. The castle's vaulted wine cellar was full of huge barrels full of vintage red wine.

Since these troops did not know how to tap these barrels, they simply shot holes into them and let the wine cascade out. It soon covered the cellar floor, then the steps and was finally four to six feet deep. The soldiers thought this to be a great joke. Many became so drunk they simply floated on a sea of wine, many of them unconscious.

Of course the next morning rumors circulated the city about free wine from the royal cellar. "Bring your buckets and fill them," was the motto. And sure enough the good citizens of Stuttgart hurried and took some of the loot. They returned home with buckets full of red wine and stories about wild-eyed and drunk occupation troops. My family did not participate in this orgy. We still had our pride.

One evening a group of drunk soldiers came to our house and rang the doorbell. They did not simply ring and let go of the bell. No, they kept their hands on our beautiful brass doorbell until Mother became disgusted and answered by opening the little glass window in our front door. Mother was not worried. She was bilingual. She spoke French as well as German. She asked the boys what they wanted, and when they yelled, "Vin, vin," she told them she was sorry but the only wine she had left was this half bottle of champagne. Since Mother approached them in a cool manner in French, they reached for the bottle, said "merci," and left.

After Stuttgart became part of the American zone, life became a little easier. We now could buy some American surplus food with our ration cards. How much we appreciated the Mixed Pickled Vegetables. Now our menu for the evening meal consisted of boiled potatoes and Mixed Pickled Vegetables, every night.

I remember when a German prisoner of war, released from a Russian prison camp, came to our door late one evening. He was starving and desperately searching for his family who had been bombed-out. He had not heard from them for a year. We invited him in and he gladly shared our meal of potatoes and mixed pickles. He thought he was in heaven. He later found his family through the Red Cross search-and-find service.

Hunger also can cause depression as well as many physical illnesses. Especially those of stomach and intestinal origin caused much suffering and death. We heard from refugees and prisoners of war that their stomachs had shrunk to the point where they could hardly eat a bite even when plenty of food was put before them. They were also too tired and too weak to continue living. We heard of much suicide out of desperation.

Lack of fat under the skin, which serves as insulation against the cold winter weather, caused other illnesses. Tuberculosis became wide spread and pneumonia took its toll. My sister Christa at age thirteen almost died of double pneumonia after having her tonsils out. She lay in the hospital for six weeks. This was the time before antibiotics were available and one had to let nature take its course.

Christa was never strong and healthy again. Her heart also was weakened. Hunger is a destructive force, but it also stirs in us the determination to survive and to hope for a future that makes life worth living again. Faith helped us to see purpose and meaning in life.

Our prayer "And give us today our daily bread" had a whole new meaning.

The CARE Package

It was 1946. CARE packages started to arrive in Germany. They were handled by the American and Swiss Red Cross. Anyone having relatives in the U.S.A. was hoping and praying for such a package. It would help to improve our diet of 1100 calories per day for quite a while. We knew of a few people who had already received CARE packages, but no one ever talked about the contents. That was a strictly kept secret.

The telephone rang. "Is this the Leonhard residence?"

"Yes, it is," Mother answered.

"There is a CARE package for you to be picked up at the gym of the Jakob School," a harsh voice shouted.

The phone connection was bad. Mother could hardly hear the man.

"A CARE package for us? Who would send us such a treasure?" We had no relatives in America.

My sister Christa and I were chosen to pick up the heaven-sent box.

"I think you need to take the wagon. The package may be too heavy for you to carry. And, anyway, it is a good half-hour walk to the Jakob School." Mother was right.

Our good old wagon had already serviced us well for many years. In peace time it had carried the baskets full of laundered sheets and tablecloths to the "mangle," where these items were pressed. During the war we pulled it up to the forest, where we collected branches and pine cones to burn for lack of coal.

And now it would have the honor of carrying this special package containing edible wonders we had never even heard of home to our waiting family.

It was a sturdy "ladder wagon." I suppose it was called that because the two long sides resembled short, wooden, varnished ladders put sideways. Front and back were connected to the sides by cross boards. Below these cross boards was open space. The spoked wooden wheels were really big. Even without a load, the wagon was heavy.

Christa and I loved it, though, because we both could ride in it. On the day of the CARE package, I folded up the old grey blanket and padded the wagon with it.

"Let's go, Christa."

"I'm coming." My sister called as she reached for her blue jacket. Christa climbed in the back of the wagon. I sat in front. Back to back we always rode down hill. Christa's legs stuck out from the back, and mine steered the handlebar in the right direction.

Down we sped on the sidewalk of Sonnenberg Strasse (Sunny Hill Road) where we lived. Our braided hair was flying in the morning wind. Through the corners of our eyes we barely noticed the rose covered, wrought iron fences of our neighbors. Faster and faster the wheels turned, louder and louder they squeaked.

"Put on the brakes, Christa," I shouted.

My sister knew just what to do. She had experience. Her feet were the brakes. She quickly bent her knees and dragged her brown leather boots along the ground until we slowed down. We had arrived at the bottom of the hill where the wagon had come to a standstill.

"This was fun, I don't think we ever went that fast."

We both took a deep breath. We climbed out and pulled the wagon across the streetcar tracks. These tracks had not been used in years. They were full of sand and weeds. We used to ride the streetcars all the time. But they and their electronic lines were destroyed by bombs. Now we had to walk and walk and walk, wherever we had to go.

Streets were easy to cross. We had only to watch out for a few American military vehicles, tanks, and jeeps. There were very few Germans who still had cars. They had been confiscated by the occupying French troops right at the end of the war. After crossing the tracks we had just a little way to go before turning a corner and arriving at a long, steep stairway.

My hometown, Stuttgart, is well known for its many stairs. These stone stairways are quite wide and are meant to be shortcuts for pedestrians.

"Let's try and take the wagon down the steps." Christa suggested.

"Yes, if we both hang on to the handlebars I think we can make it."

We turned the wagon around. It went down slowly. Bump, bump. We held tightly onto the handle and counted the steps, "Eighty-three, eighty-four, eighty-five. We made it safely.

On our way down we passed war-ruined homes, burned out shells. The Fire Station across the street from the Jakob School had been blown away by an explosive bomb. The school itself was still in bad shape. It had been sparingly repaired and had no window panes. Glass was still hard to get. The stone walls were even now covered with black soot.

Christa and I walked around the building, wagon in tow. We tried to find the entrance to the gym. That was supposed to be the place where we could pick up the CARE package. We saw no one around we could have asked for directions. Finally, we arrived at a steel door. We were familiar with these doors.

We had one installed in our house at the beginning of the war. Because the cellar was then our air raid shelter, the heavy steel door protected us from bomb splinters, debris and, air-concussion.

"This door must lead to the former air-raid shelter of the school," I said. "Let's try and open it." We pulled on the long handle and sure enough, it clicked and slowly opened. I held the heavy door while Christa pulled the wagon into the building. We walked down the dark, musty-smelling hallway. No electric lights were burning. Daylight peaked through the high, glassless window openings. We shuddered. It was cold in there, but we bravely walked on.

At the end of the hall, we turned the corner and suddenly saw a big sign saying "CARE packages this way." An arrow showed us where to go.

We arrived at a dirty looking door and knocked. Nobody answered.

"Let's go in. This is supposed to be the right place," I said and carefully opened the door. We walked in.

"Leave your wagon in the hall." This order came from an old man, dressed in grey overalls. He came shuffling towards us in old felt slippers. His glasses clung to the tip of his red nose. He stared at us.

"Christa, please stay outside in the hall and guard the wagon," I whispered and nudged my sister towards the door.

She nodded and left the room. The man took out a list of names and said, "Show me your ID card."

We never left the house without this important document. We carried it inside our clothes around our necks. After all, we were now an occupied country and could be searched by American Military Police at any given time.

While the man checked my credentials I looked around the room. The only furniture was a long, wobbly table and a folding chair on which the man sat. Behind him, stacked high, I saw many, many CARE packages. They were big, sturdy square boxes, maybe thirty by thirty inches across and twenty inches high. They all had the initials C.A.R.E. printed on top. The man lifted a box from the stack, lowered it to the floor and pushed it towards the table.

"May I help you?" I offered, but he just shook his head.

He lifted the box, our box, onto the table, took a knife and cut it open.

"I have to check the contents," he said concisely. Then he added. "It is customary for the recipient to give one item to the worker."

I was stunned! This was pure theft! I had not heard of such a rule. But then. I was just a young teenager. I did not know the new laws!

The man knew exactly what he was after. He reached for a can and pulled it out. I saw what it was—the most prized possession, a can of coffee. "Maxwell House Coffee," the label read.

"This is for me." The unpleasant man took the can and hid it under the table. I felt anger welling up in my heart, but I said nothing. That was it. Now we could take our open box and leave. I did not dare look at the contents of our precious package. That had to wait until we arrived at home.

I called Christa and she came in pulling the wagon behind her. It was up to us to lift the heavy box into the wagon. First we took the old blanket and put it on the table. Then we lifted the heavy package and carefully dropped it onto the wagon. Christa opened the blanket. She spread it over the box and tucked it in all around. No part of the box was visible.

We quickly left the school building and were on our way home. Christa pushed and I pulled until we arrived at the stairway.

"Now we have to make a decision. Either we haul the wagon up these eighty-five steps or we take the long way around the hill." I said.

Christa had an idea. "Why don't you carry the box and I will pull the wagon up the steps." It seemed very simple.

I thought about it for a while and shook my head. "I don't think so," I finally replied. "What if the box got too heavy for me and I suddenly dropped it. Everything would fall out and roll down the stairway. No, we had better take the long way home."

And so we did. I pulled, Christa pushed. Up the sidewalk, around the hill and then down again, and bump, bump across the streetcar tracks. A few persons stared at us and the wagon. They seemed to suspect we were hiding something special under that old grey blanket. They were right. But we just smiled and walked on.

Finally we arrived at home. Mother was looking for us because it had been over two hours since we left. As we came around the corner of our street, Mother waved from the balcony. She was glad to see us. Christa and I were happy, too. It was so good to be back home again with our package.

Mother met us at the gate. "I can tell you have that CARE package under the blanket," she laughed.

"Mother, that grumpy old man opened our box and stole a big can of coffee. He was really mean." Christa burst out angrily.

"Well, let's hope he will enjoy the coffee as much as we would have." Mother was in a forgiving mood. But I could tell by her voice that she would have thoroughly enjoyed and appreciated a cup of "real" coffee, not the "ersatzkaffee" made of roasted grain and chicory we had gotten used to.

We hauled the package up the outside kitchen steps and carefully placed it onto the kitchen table. Thank goodness, the hauling, lifting, and pulling were finally over. Our muscles ached, and I had blisters on my hands from pulling the wagon. "Ouch." But I did not complain.

"Oh Mother, may we please open it right away?" Christa was getting really excited. She could not wait any longer. She had to find out what was in that big, heavy box.

"Of course," Mother smiled. She pulled out a big sack of flour, then sugar and cornmeal.

"Oh look, this can says Hershey's Cocoa."

"And here, look, these are chocolate bars. They are called Oh Henry. What a funny name for chocolate." We had found some real treasures.

We unpacked other foods like a can of pork in raisin sauce,

some cake mixes, and a big box of Velveeta Cheese. The cheese had started to form mold, but we just scraped it clean and ate it anyway. We were overwhelmed. The kitchen table was full of things we had never heard of. We were getting hungry just thinking about trying all this good food.

Among the new food was peanut butter, condensed milk, and tea bags. We had already opened the can of pork loin. The meat was delicious, but why the raisin sauce? We had never heard of any meat/fruit combination. No problem, we heated up the sauce until it became a liquid. We carefully fished the raisins from the gravy, rinsed them well in a sieve, dried them in the warm oven, and used them in Mother's coffee cake. Wonderful.

Tea bags were not that easy to figure out. "Lipton Tea," the label read. I pulled one of these little white bags out of the box and held it up high.

What was this? I smelled it and then tried to find an opening in the tea bag. My efforts were in vain, there was no opening. I handed it to Mother. She was puzzled, too.

"Americans are known to be such practical people. Why on earth do they put their tea leaves in these little bags with no openings. How are we supposed to get the tea out?"

"Wait just a minute, I have an idea that may work." I ran and took my nail scissors from my night table and cut the tea bag down the middle.

"There. That must be the way the Americans get their tea out."

Christa was not impressed. "But the tea leaves are so tiny they will go through our tea strainer and will end up in our cups."

We sighed, we did not understand.

We shrugged off the problem with the tea bags and begged Mother to open the can of Sweetened Condensed Milk.

We were familiar with Kondensierte Milch. It was evaporated. The English word 'condensed' sounded similar to German.

"It must be the same thing. It says so here in the dictionary." I had it all figured out. English had been my favorite subject all through the war, and now I could use what I had learned.

But after Mother opened the can, we all stood and stared at the thick, yellowish, pudding-like paste. This was quite unexpected.

"Well," I said. "Obviously, there is a difference sometimes between British and American English." We had studied the pure Queen's Oxford English.

We passed the can around.

"It smells really delicious." I sounded encouraging.

I dipped a tea spoon into the sweet smelling mixture. Mother and my sisters watched me. With the tip of my tongue I tasted the condensed milk.

"Oh, this is really good. It even has a slight vanilla taste." I felt goose bumps creeping up my neck. I had not expected such culinary delight to ever touch my taste buds. Now everyone tasted a tiny bit of this wonderful treat.

Mother was thrilled. "Let's cover the can and wait till tomorrow morning. Then we will use it in our coffee. I can hardly wait. It will make the ersatzkaffee taste just delicious."

We dreamed about it all night. The only fresh milk we could buy then with our ration cards was bluish, watery skim milk. Only expecting and nursing mothers and infants were issued whole milk.

The next morning we got up bright and early and stood around the kitchen. I ground the grain coffee, Mother sprinkled it over the boiling water, stirred it, turned off the gas and added a spoonful of chicory. After we waited three minutes, the coffee grounds had settled.

"So, now hand me your cups and I will fill them," Mother was ready.

One by one we stirred a spoonful of condensed milk into our coffee. We kept stirring and stirring, but the sweet paste remained stuck to our spoons. I watched the others, but they had the same problem as I. I finally took my spoon out of my cup and licked it clean. So did the others. We were disappointed.

"Well," said Mother, "the only thing I can think of is to use the milk as a sandwich spread. Maybe that is what the Americans do."

So we did. And oh did we love those sandwiches.

Peanut butter was another puzzle. The only way we had tasted peanuts was to eat them right out of the shells. They were imported items and we had not seen them for many years. But we had good memories of them. We loved their taste, but what we liked most of all was the fact that we could open them without a nutcracker. The only nuts native to Germany were hazelnuts and English walnuts. Both had hard shells and when we used the nutcracker we often got our hands pinched. That hurt.

Mother was quite protective of the jar of peanut butter that looked and smelled so inviting. Any kind of fat was still rationed and very scarce.

Mother announced cheerfully. "Tonight we shall have lovely fried potatoes for supper. This peanut butter will surely melt like any other butter. The potatoes will get a beautiful brown crust and we all will love them."

Oh, we had faint memories of potatoes and onions sizzling in the frying pan, their aroma filling the kitchen, but that was long ago. For many years we had to cook our potatoes without oil. We added a little water to the potatoes in the frying pan and waited until a light brown crust formed. We had to watch the dish carefully, though, because the potatoes had a tendency to burn.

Supper time was near. We peeled the potatoes, while Mother sliced them. We were all set to test the peanut butter. Mother happily scooped a big spoonful of it into the frying pan. She turned on the gas, and we watched the big brown blob. It just sat there.

"It probably needs more heat," I suggested.

Mother turned up the gas burner.

"We have to be patient."

We tried to be.

Suddenly, Christa jumped up and down in excitement.

"Look, it is starting to melt."

We looked closer. She was right. A tiny puddle of oil was seeping from the blob.

"It is melting. Look, it is melting."

We fixed our wide open eyes on the peanut butter. But the little puddle of oil did not get any bigger, or the brown blob any smaller.

"Something is not right," Mother sighed.

The melted oil began to smoke. Mother scooped the brown blob out of the pan and onto a plate.

We shook our heads. We could not figure out why it would not melt.

"But I see enough oil in the pan to fry the potatoes." I was quite optimistic.

And so we had fried potatoes. They tasted different, but heavenly just the same.

After that we had fried potatoes until the peanut butter jar was empty. The brown part that did not melt was scooped up out of the frying pan every time and carefully dropped in a jar. It was brown, dry, and crumbly, but with a knife in hand we pushed it onto slices of black bread and thinly covered it with sweetened condensed milk. What a treat. We had no jam or honey, and Mother told us that peanut butter would stick to the roof of our mouths if eaten alone. She was right. We had tried it..

The combination of lovely sweet milk and peanut butter was just perfect. Too bad it did not last very long.

One evening my sisters and I were busy helping Mother tear open all the Lipton tea bags and drop their contents into an empty tin. Father arrived home from work at the hospital and was pleased to see us busy.

He announced, "I received a letter today from an old school friend who had emigrated to the U.S.A. as a very young man. He had searched for our address, and having not found it, he sent the letter to the hospital. He was the dear person who sent us the CARE package. We had lost contact with him during the war. How can we ever thank him."

Many years later my parents visited this childhood friend and his family in their lovely home in Philadelphia, Pennsylvania. Had it not been for war and CARE packages, they may have never been able to renew their friendship.

It was quite some time before we found out that tea bags do not have to be torn open before use and that peanut butter is not for frying potatoes. We all had a good laugh about it and never forgot our experiences with our first CARE package.

CARE stands for: Cooperative American Remittances to Europe.

The Winter of 1947

The winter of 1947 was the hardest to live through since World War Two began in 1939. There was no peace treaty, although the war had ended two and a half years earlier. Life was becoming increasingly difficult.

Our beloved Stuttgart remained in ruins and food was still rationed. We lived on eleven hundred calories a day—a starvation diet, but worse was the fact that our money had such little value.

Everyone who had anything left had to barter things to survive. Mother put an ad in the newspaper saying, "Dolls and doll carriages, hand painted mocca service and toys traded for ladies clothes."

I was shocked when I read the ad. The beautiful china mocca service had been a Christmas present years ago. My sisters and I used it for tea parties with our friends. The dolls and carriages had long been packed away in the attic. We had outgrown playing with childish toys, but we were still attached to them. We never dreamed of a day when we would have to let go of our precious childhood memories by trading them for clothing. It must have been hard for Mother, too.

I remember people lining up in front of the house early in the morning after reading the ad in the paper. Mother let each woman come in separately, showed her the toys, and looked at the clothes she had to offer in return.

In the end, Mother traded our building blocks and games as well. She felt so sorry for the young mothers who had no toys for their children.

Later that morning, after everything had been traded, a nanny, who worked for a neighbor family, came by to look at the doll carriages, but the carriages were long gone. Mother was sorry.

The nanny said, "I am sorry to be late. You could have seen me taking walks past your house with the little girls pushing your carriages. You would have seen how well we took care of them."

We all would have liked that.

I do not recall what the traded clothes looked like other than some satin slips and cotton blouses. What I do remember is that none of us three girls had any warm sweaters and skirts to wear. I had already unraveled all the knitted baby clothes that Mother had kept. The yarn was so thin. I had to use three or four strands together for knitting my sweater. Someone had told me that gauze bandages could also be used and since we had plenty of those I added a few rows to the front of my creation. It really looked good and I was very proud of it.

For a pattern I had used an old, small sweater and just added a few inches on all sides. No problem. My sisters just shook their heads and walked by me as I earnestly knitted away. They would have never dreamed of doing what I did.

Mother had taken some sturdy, white linen sheets and made us summer dresses. She even embroidered the collars and sleeve cuffs. We did not like these dresses. They were stiff and wrinkled terribly. We wore them anyway with no complaints.

Then a miracle happened. We received a package from Switzerland. It contained three sweaters and three skirts for my sisters and I, as well as dried fruit, flour, sugar and coffee. The package had come to us through the Lutheran Church of America. We were so touched by the goodness of people we did not know. They were angels sent from heaven who saved our lives. We all knelt down and said a thank you prayer. It was an experience we would never have had without this terrible war.

"It is more blessed to give than to receive," the saying goes, but learning to receive when we were always used to giving made us more sensitive to the feelings of our needy fellow men.

Heating materials were another problem. Central heating was impossible. We were able to install small woodburning stoves in two rooms. Through the Forestry Department we were able to secure a war-damaged tree in the woods. It was marked by a ribbon and a number and became our tree. Nobody else could touch it!

How we would fell it and transport it home was our problem. The Forestry Department did not provide these services. Luckily we could engage a man with a saw and truck who delivered the logs to our house. We all helped to carry the heavy pieces up the twenty steps from the street to our back yard. Father split the logs and we stacked them in the wood cellar. We also gathered splinters of wood in abandoned ruins of homes and used them for kindling. The splinters helped to start the fires in the stoves because the wood was old and dry and did not smoke.

All school rooms now had stoves with pipes out the windows. Each student was assigned a day when she had to bring enough fire wood to heat the classroom sparingly for four hours. When the fire went out, it was the end of the school day. We never took off our coats and mittens while in class.

The rest of the day was spent doing plenty of homework. The warmest spots in our home were our beds. Mother would fix each of us a warm water bottle for our cold feet and we were quite comfortable. We spent a lot of time in bed the winter of

1947. After finishing our homework we would read, play cards, or practice our wooden flutes.

Of course, after a good snowfall, we went skiing, sledding, or skating, We always made the best of a bad situation. Our lives did not improve until 1948 when we finally received our new money. Then slowly the economy started up again and the Marshall Plan helped us to rebuild our country, but we were still occupied by foreign troops and divided into four different zones which we could not cross without Permits.

Currency Reform from
Rentenmark to Deutschemark

We knew it was coming. We realized that our Rentenmark (RM) had lost its value. After a devastating world war this was to be expected.

Before 1918 the currency was called Reichsmark. Its value was based to a high percentage on gold. These gold bars were kept in bank vaults. No private person was permitted to horde gold. Gold coins were taken out of circulation.

The Reichsmark was steadily devalued after World War I. A catastrophic depression followed that war, lost by Germany. Mother told me, "The money lost value daily in the 1920s. Finally it became hard to have enough money to buy even a loaf of bread. The worst I remember came when we had to pay one million Reichsmark for bread. When the new currency was given out, one million Reichsmark became one Rentenmark."

The Rentenmark was mainly based on the value of real estate, natural resources, exports, and what we call Gross National Product (the total monetary value of all goods and services produced in a country during one year). A small percentage of the Rentenmark was still based on gold. (Toward the end of the second world war many German banks sent their gold bars to Switzerland for safe keeping.)

After the total destruction and division of Germany in 1945, we wondered what the new currency would be based on. Real estate was destroyed, and areas rich in natural resources were annexed to other countries. The rich agricultural state of Prussia was given to Poland, the areas of Silesia and other Eastern German states with valuable resources in minerals became part of the Soviet Union, and in the West the Saarland, rich in coal, was annexed to France.

What would this new money look like? Could we trust it to be stable and become a world currency or would it be worthless paper? If we could only take a glance into the future. Of course we could not and so all we could do was hope for the best.

From my war diary:

June 1, 1948
A few stores are open again in Stuttgart. Most of them are temporary huts in the midst of ruins. The streets are partially cleared of rubble. These new shops are mostly owned by foreign people who do not want to return to their homeland in Eastern Europe. They are afraid of the Russians who are now occupying their countries. Several million of these people are now living in West Germany. They are called Displaced Persons. They have special privileges and want to eventually live in the U.S.A. They dress differently and speak languages we do not understand.

Those Germans whose homes were not destroyed in the war have to make room for the displaced persons as well as other refugees. It is hard to share close quarters with them, especially kitchens and bathrooms. We hope this is not forever.

June 21, 1948

   Now the chaos of last week is over. We were told that the new currency would have only one fifth of the present money's worth. People went berserk buying anything just to use up as much as possible of the old Rentenmarks. We had lots and lots of this now worthless paper money and very few goods to buy.

   I walked downtown to see what I could get for my pocketful of "paper." The prices had been raised sky high. Nobody cared. In front of all open stores people stood in long lines. I joined a group at the entrance to a drugstore. I wondered what they had to sell. I saw people come out of this store with their trophies, namely old perfume, lipstick, and fabric flowers. All worthless stuff.

   By the time I was finally waited on only moth crystals were left. I bought some. Mother was delighted.

   All food stores are closed until Monday, June 22nd. Today is Sunday. We went to church this morning in our new Barrack Church. It was consecrated last week. Our Zion's Kirche was destroyed by fire bombs in 1943. After that our youth group met each week in the ruin. We brought our hammers and chipped away on the brown bricks to clear them of mortar. We hope we can rebuild our church some time in the future. For five years small groups of church members met in homes for worship.

   We are thankful to the American Lutheran Church who arranged for a Swiss company to send us building materials pre-cut, with instructions. We even received a piano, our lovely pipe organ in the old church had burned in 1943.

   After Sunday dinner I took the fifteen-minute walk down the hill to the Wilhelm's Boys High School. My parents were glad that I had volunteered for the task of getting our new money. I had to stay in line at the school for exactly two hours, from 1:30 to 3:30 p.m. All people had their 300 Rentenmarks in hand. That was the amount we had to turn in before receiving the new Deutschemarks.

   Standing in line was entertaining. People had a lot of sarcastic humor. They made fun of the new currency, wondering if it would improve our economy. "The old money is now good only for toilet paper, ha, ha, ha . . ." one man shouted.

"Or to paper our walls," yelled another. Everyone laughed.

When it was my turn to hand over the old Marks I received 200 DM, forty for each family member. It felt strange to finger these brand new bank notes colored blue, pink, and green. Each denomination has a different color and size, easy to distinguish from each other. Coins are not available yet, instead we use the old one Mark note. (1 Mark equals now 10 Pfennig.)

On this day, June 21, 1948, all people had the same amount of money, namely 40 Deutschemark, (about $10). All stores were closed. The next morning a few stores opened.

Frau Schatzmann who lives across from us asked us to come by her store and see her lovely leather ware. She must have stored these items until the new money came into circulation. Of course we have no money for such luxuries right now. We have to learn to be thrifty.

Our savings accounts cannot be touched yet. Not enough money has been printed. We wonder how we will adjust to this new system. I feel sorry for people with no jobs. But our finance minister Koehler said. "Fear not, he who works will live." This is our consolation."

As Germany rebuilt its economy thanks to the Marshall Plan, factories produced items for export only. We visited exhibits of fine china, crystal, leather, jewelry, fabrics and furniture. We could admire everything, but we could not buy these items for years to come.

Now the Deutschemark is one of the most sought after international currencies. The cities are rebuilt and new generations of German youth are growing up in comfort and affluence which we, who grew up and suffered through World War Two, could only dream of. We all pray for peace to last forever.

Swiss Franks and Other "Forbidden Fruit"

The stable Swiss Francs have always been a very sought after currency. Swiss bank accounts are favored by the world's wealthiest people. These accounts are often used as tax shelters and are only known by their numbers. Names or countries of origin are not known. Swiss banks do not give interest on these foreign accounts, but they are tax free.

The monies or such valuables as gold are locked away in secret vaults of the Swiss National Bank. The "Gnomes of Zurich," as the bankers are called, keep their eyes shut, their ears closed, and their mouths zipped. "See no evil, hear no evil, speak no evil."

After World War II Germans were not allowed to own any foreign currencies, including Pounds Sterling, Dollars, Swiss Francs or others. Needless to say this gave rise to Black Market deals especially in Swiss Francs. After all, Switzerland is

Germany's nextdoor neighbor to the Southwest. Also forbidden to be taken across the border were American cigarettes, coffee, and Swiss chocolates. I remember when I crossed over into Switzerland in 1950. I had been engaged by a Swiss family to be the intern-governess for their two children. I needed this experience as part of my education, with the goal of becoming a Developmental Psychologist. I was all set. I had my passport and visa for one year. I had purchased my train ticket with German money. It read "Stuttgart Zurich-Chur."

"Once you are across the border in Switzerland, surely you will be able to exchange some of your German money into Swiss Francs," some well-traveled friends of my parents suggested.

But when I arrived in Chur, no one wanted my Deutschemarks and I needed to take the postauto bus to Trin Mulin up in the mountains. The Swiss family had its summer home in that charming little town. I was desperate. Luckily the kind bus driver understood my dilemma and let me ride with him free of charge.

Before crossing the German-Swiss border by train, I had an experience I shall never forget.

Schaffhausen is the border town, part German, part Swiss. All German passengers who were traveling to Swiss destinations had to leave the German train with their suitcases and stand in line to have their passports and luggage checked. I was not concerned. I had a good conscience. I was honest. I was not going to smuggle anything across the border. I was willing to let the border control check my suitcase. I had nothing to hide.

While standing in line, a German police woman in a white coat pulled me out of the line of passengers and said, "Take your suitcase and follow me."

I had no idea why I was chosen. Maybe I would receive some special treatment. The woman in white took me to a small, dark room in the back of the train station and began to ask me questions.

"Why are you leaving the country? Are you taking anything illegal with you? Do you have relatives in Switzerland?" And on she went.

I answered a fervent "No" to all these questions. Then she searched my suitcase but found only clothes. I was relieved and expected to rejoin my fellow passengers. But no . . .

"Take off your coat and shoes," she ordered.

She checked the shoulder padding and lining of my coat. She reached into my shoes then shook them. Nothing fell out.

"Open your blouse."

Terror struck me as I opened the buttons.

What on Earth is this person looking for, I thought.

She reached inside my bra. Next she fingered through my hair. My handbag was the last thing she turned upside down.

"You can get dressed now," she said nonchalantly.

The examination seemed to have taken forever. Through the small window of the room I could watch my fellow passengers climbing back on the train. The two German coaches had been hooked onto a Swiss engine and we were to leave from the Swiss side of the station.

What if the train were to leave without me? What if I would miss my connection in Zurich? I would then possibly be too late for the bus and would not make it to Trin Mulin. And I had no Swiss coins to even contact the family expecting me. My wandering thoughts made me very uneasy.

"You may pack your suitcase now and leave." The white-coated woman said simply.

But I needed to know why I had to endure such an extensive search. While folding my clothes and stacking them back into my case, I asked the obvious question. "Please tell me why I was picked for this thorough search. What were you looking for?"

"Well, sometimes the most harmless people are suspect and guilty of illegal activities," she said. "I am looking for smugglers of Swiss Francs."

Hmmm, I thought. If I ever wanted to illegally take Swiss money across the border I surely would know where not to hide it.

When I returned to Germany six months later, something funny happened on the way to the Swiss-German border. I sat as the only woman in a train compartment for eight passengers, a comfortable, quiet Swiss train with an electric engine. No one spoke on the trip between Zurich and Schaffhausen. I looked around me. Everyone was busy hiding behind a newspaper or book. I had a window seat. The well dressed gentleman in gray across from me occasionally nibbled on some obviously American salted peanuts. He had placed the can on the little tray table by the window.

Next to him sat a man whom I could only identify as such because of his trousers and manly shoes. His huge newspaper, the *Zuricher Zeitung* covered the rest of his body completely. His raincoat dangled from the hook next to him.

In the corner by the compartment door, a portly man had taken a seat at the last moment before the train left the station in Zurich. He had a round, reddish face, and held the very popular book *Gone With the Wind* in his pudgy hands. I had read this book in German and seen the movie twice in English — with German subtitles.

The rhythm of the moving train made me sleepy and I dozed off for a little while.

"Tickets and passports, please." The Swiss conductor in his gray uniform and hat opened the compartment door. I sleepily reached for my purse and showed him the requested documents.

"Thank you." The conductor said before he went on to the next compartment.

The German border policeman entered. "Does anyone carry any cigarettes, coffee, or chocolates? Swiss Francs?" He looked sternly at all the passengers.

This would be the last chance to confess. We all knew the law.

"No," we all shook our heads.

"You, sir, please open your case." The policeman was suspicious.

The man with the raincoat folded his huge newspaper, sighed, and reached for his small overnight case in the rack above him. He fiddled with the keys but finally opened the bag. It was full of cigarettes. Not in packages or cartons, no, I saw rows and rows of carefully stacked white, fragrant cigarettes. I could not believe my eyes. I was embarrassed and angry at the same time. Surely, this man knew the law, yet he had taken a chance of getting caught smuggling this sought after commodity, American cigarettes.

He had probably planned to barter them on the Black Market. The train had now come to a stop at the Swiss border.

"Close your case and follow me," was the policeman's order.

The two men left the train.

Our coach was switched to a German steam engine and left for Germany. We never saw the smuggler again. His raincoat still dangled from the hook.

Suddenly all passengers put away their reading materials and started to smile and talk to each other. They were now free to confess. No more searches had to be feared.

The portly man with the reddish face broke the silence. "My Swiss friends wrapped everything in decorative paper to make it look like these were some birthday presents. They even wrote fictitious names on each item. I believe these packages contain cigarettes, coffee, and Swiss chocolate." He laughed out loud. He seemed happy about having fooled the authorities. "Ha, I outsmarted the police."

"I was even more clever," smiled the well dressed man across from me.

"I hid one thousand Swiss Francs tightly folded in the bottom of my can of peanuts. Right here on the tray table in full sight of everybody."

It became clear to me, the innocent one, that the more openly one "hides" the smuggled goods the less they are discovered.

"You gave me ideas for my next trip across the border," mumbled another passenger.

Forbidden fruit is so sweet, I thought.

Arriving in the New World.

Three and a half days had passed since we left Le Havre, France. This fastest of all passenger ships had nearly *flown* across the Atlantic in the shortest time ever. Every night we had turned our watches back two hours, and now, as we approached our destination, we were on perfect New York time. We had crossed six time zones.

At five o'clock that morning we were awakened by three bass-toned blasts of the ships horns.

"We are about to sail past the Statue of Liberty and soon we will land in the harbor of New York," the captain announced in his calm, low voice.

I rubbed my eyes and slipped down from my upper bunk. I peeped through the round porthole, the cabin's window. Dawn was near. The morning clouds had taken on a pale pink glow.

"I can hardly believe we have arrived. Is it really true that we are in America?" I pinched myself. Yes, this was reality not just a pleasant dream.

My two cabin mates had already gone on deck. I hurriedly dressed and reached for my little box camera. This historic moment of passing the Statue of Liberty had to be captured in photos.

Out of breath I reached the upper deck. Most of the two thousand passengers had already assembled there. Everyone stood in awe. What a grand sight: Liberty herself, her strong arm stretched high toward heaven, her torch lit—welcomed us.

The ship's horns once more gave three blasts as we silently and reverently past by this famous landmark. The sky's colors had changed from hues of pale pink to bright red and purple, and in the foreground we now recognized the contours of the skyscrapers of Manhattan.

Our glorious ship, the S.S. United States had arrived at her goal. Her noisy engines had stopped. Tugboats safely guided her now to her berth.

This was August 28, 1954. It was the first day of my year as a college student in the United States. This year changed my life forever.